CROWDED HOUSE

SONG BY SONG

CROWDED HOUSE

SONG BY SONG

Paul Clark

FONTHILL

First published in Great Britain in 2026 by
Fonthill
An imprint of
Pen & Sword Books Ltd
Yorkshire – Philadelphia

ISBN 978-1-03615-677-0

A CIP catalogue record for this book is available from the British Library.

Typeset by Simon and Sons ITES Services Pvt. Ltd., Chennai, India.
Printed and bound in the UK by CPI Group (UK) Ltd, Croydon, CR0 4YY

FSC www.fsc.org
MIX
Paper | Supporting responsible forestry
FSC® C013604

The Publisher's authorised representative in the EU for product safety is Authorised Rep Compliance Ltd., Ground Floor, 71 Lower Baggot Street, Dublin D02 P593, Ireland.
www.arccompliance.com

For a complete list of Pen & Sword titles please contact

PEN & SWORD BOOKS LIMITED
47 Church Street, Barnsley, South Yorkshire, S70 2AS, England
E-mail: enquiries@pen-and-sword.co.uk
Website: www.pen-and-sword.co.uk
or
PEN AND SWORD BOOKS
1950 Lawrence Road, Havertown, PA 19083, USA
E-mail: uspen-and-sword@casematepublishers.com
Website: www.penandswordbooks.com

Preface

While researching the career of Crowded House for this book, I have had the opportunity to reflect on my relationship with the band and when I first discovered them. In my mid-teens, I probably heard 'Don't Dream It's Over' being played on the radio. There might have been some mention of the band in the music press. At the time, it may have passed me by that they were an Australian/New Zealand band; their slick videos may have led me to think of them as another US band MTV had on heavy rotation. Given that they came and went so quickly, I may have dismissed them as one-hit wonders, never to be heard of again.

'Don't Dream It's Over' was not the big hit it should have been in the UK. The song only reached number 27 in the charts in 1986. It was a bigger hit elsewhere in the world. Inexplicably, a Paul Young cover version charted seven places higher at number 20 in 1991. Ironically, that cover version was probably instrumental in helping the band gain more fans. Crowded House re-released 'Don't Dream It's Over' as a single in the UK in 1996, as part of the *Recurring Dream* promotion. It peaked at number 25 on that occasion, still not higher than the Paul Young version.

Despite a reputation for writing perfect pop songs, as a singles band, Crowded House did not take off in the UK until the 'Fall at Your Feet' single in 1991. It is always a good feeling when you discover what you think to be a 'new' band and find that they have already amassed a healthy back catalogue of a couple of albums and several singles to go back and listen to. Then you find out that Neil Finn was a member of Split Enz. That opens up another treasure trove of great tunes.

My relationship with the band started around the release of *Woodface*, and I have not looked back since. This book has allowed me to reflect on the career of Crowded House, particularly its principal songwriter, Neil Finn. I have been able to look back on their albums and listen to favourites again and rediscover songs that I may have overlooked down the years.

Given the longevity of a band's career, there can be allowances for when the great heights of previous albums have not been achieved with subsequent releases. Having completed the book, I do not think that the band's standards have dropped significantly at any point. There has been a high level of consistency along the way. *Woodface* holds a special place in my heart, as it was the first album I bought on the day of release. If I were to say that I had a favourite album, it would be *Together Alone*. That is the album that I find myself returning to over and over again. There is something complete about that collection of songs. In this age of playlists and shuffling music, it is an album that should be listened to without skipping, but more on that later.

While writing the book, I have found it hard not to equate the skills of Neil Finn as a songwriter with another band that is amongst my favourites, The Beatles. It may seem that the description of 'Beatlesque' could be seen as a copout when it is hard to be descriptive of the talents of Neil Finn. I do not do this lightly; I think Neil Finn has the right to be discussed in these terms, given his exceptional ear for melody that has served him well down the years.

Bill Drummond of the KLF and previously a manager of Echo & the Bunnymen was once asked why so many great bands came out of Mathew Street, Liverpool, the place where The Cavern and Eric's club are situated. He wanted to avoid the usual pat answer of it being about the docks, he pointed to something more mystical:

> It is the interstellar ley line. It comes careering in from outer space, hits the world in Iceland, bounces back up, writhing about like a conger eel, then down Mathew Street in Liverpool where the Cavern Club—and latterly Eric's—is. Back up, twisting, turning, wriggling across the face of the earth until it reaches the uncharted mountains of New Guinea, where it shoots back into space. Deep space. You know what ley lines are? Those things that hippies are into, imaginary power lines across ancient Britain, lines that can be traced by Saxon churches, stone circles, burial mounds, that sort of stuff. But just boringly straight and static. Well, this interstellar ley line is a mega-powered one. The only three fixed points on earth it travels through are Iceland, Mathew Street in Liverpool and New Guinea. Wherever something creatively or spiritually mega happens anywhere else on earth, it is because this interstellar ley line is momentarily powering through the territory.[1]

If you believe that explanation, I would say that he underestimated the length of that ley line and that it could be said to stretch as far as Te Awamutu, New Zealand.

Another observation that rings true comes from the writer and friend of Neil Finn, Pete Paphides, who remembered a comment someone once made about the songs of Crowded House in a *Record Collector* interview in 2024. He said that 'anyone even passingly familiar with their body of work will know that beneath the surface of every one of their songs seemingly built for mass participation—"Don't Dream It's Over", "Weather With You", "Fall At Your Feet", "Better Be Home Soon"—lurk deeper undercurrents of melancholy that, decades previously, saw some perceptive wag label Finn's songwriting style as "Leonard [Cohen] and McCartney".'[2]

As I am a UK-based writer, there is some inevitability that this book will be written from a UK perspective. I am aware that discussions about hits (and misses) might have different perspectives in certain territories. Although I have taken into account the comparative chart positions elsewhere, particularly for Australia, New Zealand, and the US, for the book.

Acknowledgements

I would like to thank Jay Slater and the team at Fonthill Media for allowing me to spend time indulging myself with the music of Crowded House. It has been time well spent.

I would also like to thank my wife, Vivienne, for letting me dictate the playlists in our house while writing this book. It was all in the name of research. She is now an avid fan, despite maybe wanting to hear something other than the subject of this book over the last few months. Notably, we had one of our first dates at a Crowded House gig in Manchester, and a more recent date night took place during their tour warm-up in Liverpool's Cavern Club in 2024.

This book is dedicated to the memory of Mum, Joan and Dad, Barry. They are much missed.

Contents

Introduction

In an alternate universe, this could have been a book about the continued presence of Split Enz, the progressive-art-rockers formed in 1972 in New Zealand by Tim Finn—a band that would eventually include the talents of Finn's younger brother, Neil, as a co-singer and songwriter. It was Neil's contributions that saw the band shift from a respected cult act to one that gained wider international attention. 'Message to My Girl' was the song that had crossover appeal. This was also a foretaste of the musical style and ear for melody that have become the standard for Neil Finn.

Having become the principal member of that band, Neil decided to change streams and start again under a new band name, albeit with members who had previously served with the Split Enz. 'Then I was faced with the choice of, well, do I keep going in this band, and as a lead singer? But it just seemed too intimidating, and I wanted to strike out.'[1]

It was a case of starting again. With a new identity, without the baggage of Split Enz. Neil expressed his thoughts on the new outfit to *Musician Magazine* at the time of the release of *Woodface*: 'Paul had just joined the band, and he was about my age. I began to revel in the idea of having a small group of guys about my age.'[2]

It is unlikely this would have been a book about The Party Boys, a ramshackle cover band Neil joined that briefly toured the pubs of New Zealand. It was never going to be about The Mullanes either. The latter was a short-lived name derived from the middle name of frontman Neil Finn. The Mullanes' debut gig was on the Coaster-to-Coaster tour of Australia, at the Arts Factory in Byron Bay on 21 May 1985. Neil Finn, Paul Hester, Nick Seymour and Craig Hooper were the band that day. The record label subsequently dissuaded the band from using that name.

Instead, this is a book about Crowded House and their continued success as a band nearly four decades after their formation.

The band has had several distinct phases. The first is the ascent. The eponymous debut album in 1986 was successful in the US, Australia and New Zealand. The follow-up album, *Temple of Low Men*, was released in 1988.

The UK had been slow to embrace the charms of Crowded House. The *Woodface* album in 1991 changed the band's fortunes. The *Together Alone* album of 1993 saw the band retreat to Neil Finn's homeland to record their most accomplished record.

The first era of the band concluded with the homecoming *Farewell to the World* concert on the steps of the Sydney Opera House in 1996. This was initially released on VHS, before a CD and DVD release in 2006.

With the band no more, Neil Finn pursued a solo career that includes some notable collaborations. He has embraced differing styles. At times, his music can be seen as more experimental in comparison to the early songs of Crowded House.

Paul Hester went on to pursue a career as a TV presenter. Nick Seymour moved to Ireland, where he developed a passion for art. He also got involved with music production.

The second phase of the band starts with the *Time on Earth* album in 2007. It was initially meant to be the third solo album from Neil Finn. The band was brought back together following the untimely death of Paul Hester. The album takes on a reflective tone as a result of the loss of their friend and former colleague.

Since then, they have added to that back catalogue with three more studio albums: *Intriguer* (2010), *Dreamers Are Waiting* (2020) and *Gravity Stairs* (2024).

The *Dreamers Are Waiting* album is the album that heralded the third phase of the band, as the line-up of the band changed once more. In came Neil Finn's sons, Elroy and Liam. They also welcomed back an old friend from the early days of the band, producer Mitchell Froom. He now took on the role of the band's keyboardist.

While Crowded House has continued to evolve, Neil Finn has carved out a successful solo career in tandem with the 'day job'. He even took the time to join Fleetwood Mac in 2018 for a world tour and became a member of the band until they disbanded. In 2026, he rejoined Split Enz for a series of gigs to celebrate the re-release of a number of the band's classic albums.

After eight studio albums and numerous compilations and live records, Crowded House is one of the most respected bands around today. They are still producing music and touring the world and gathering new fans along the way.

This book explores the stories behind each album and other aspects of Neil Finn's career.

1

Crowded House (1986)

Original album release:	June 1986
5.1 surround DVD-Audio release:	July 2002
Deluxe Edition release:	November 2016
Personnel:	Neil Finn: guitar, piano and lead vocals Paul Hester: drums and background vocals Nick Seymour: bass guitar Tim Pierce: guitar Jim Keltner: drums on 'Now We're Getting Somewhere' Jerry Scheff: bass on 'Now We're Getting Somewhere' Noël: backing vocals Jim Gilstrap: backing vocals Andy Milton: backing vocals Joe Satriani: backing vocals Jorge Bermudez: backing vocals Heart Attack Horns: backing vocals Mitchell Froom: keyboards
Duration:	38:40
Recorded at:	Capitol Recording Studios, Los Angeles and Sunset Sound Factory, Los Angeles, and Platinum Studios, Melbourne
Produced by:	Mitchell Froom, except 'Can't Carry On' was produced by Eddie Rayner and Neil Finn at Platinum Studios, Melbourne
Engineers:	Tchad Blake, Dennis Kirk
Chart positions:	Australia: 1; New Zealand: 3; US: 12; UK: 99

One thing was certain in the mind of Neil Finn following the demise of Split Enz: he wanted to continue working with Paul Hester, the band's latter-day drummer. He also knew that he wanted to work in a band setting again; this time, it would be more manageable than the way Split Enz operated. The option of a solo career was not off the table as he worked out his next steps.

The initial demos of the new project he worked on with Paul were done at Osborne Street, in the Melbourne suburb of South Yarra. The plan was to audition bassists by getting them to work with the demos. While the songs were not fully formed at this stage, they were substantial enough to give would-be bassists an idea of what was needed. One of the songs that formed part of the initial demos was 'Walking on the Spot'. The demo version can be found on the 2016 deluxe edition of *Crowded House*.

There were two contenders for the role of bass player. First was Bones Hillman, who would go on to have a long stint working with Midnight Oil. He contributed a bassline to 'Can't Carry On', which made it onto the first album.[1] But it was felt his style of playing was too similar to that of Nigel Griggs, previously of Split Enz.

Nick Seymour was selected because he played well on 'That's What I Call Love', his funky bass style was different to what Neil Finn first thought he wanted. Neil Finn gave Paul Hester the casting vote: 'What do you reckon, Bones or Nick?' I put the word in for Nick.'[2]

The band were looking beyond New Zealand and Australia for a record deal. It was by chance that someone who could help them with that ambition was on vacation in New Zealand. Gary Stamler, a music attorney from Los Angeles, fortuitously read about the demise of Split Enz. The band happened to be playing one of their final gigs that night. He had heard a few things from them and went out to see them. He snapped up one of the last remaining tickets.

When he got there, he was taken by the talents of Neil Finn and his potential to be an international star. He altered his close friend Tom Whalley, who was an A&R guy for Warner Bros. Records. He was interested in hearing demos from the band. Tapes went back and forth, and it was the second tape that clinched the deal. This contained basic versions of 'Don't Dream It's Over', plus 'Love You 'til the Day I Die', 'Hole in the River' and the chorus of 'Now We're Getting Somewhere'.

Whalley was very impressed by what he heard, but then he got a phone call which cooled his interest a little. A prominent player in Australian music publishing called to say he had seen a couple of gigs by The Mullanes, and advised Whalley not to go near the group, as 'they weren't very good.'[3]

Still needing convincing, Tom Whalley flew over to see the band play in Melbourne, but was still uncertain by what he saw live. Capitol Records was looking to expand its international roster of artists, and this may have convinced them to take a risk with the band. EMI Australia would underwrite this to a certain extent.

The band was still evolving at the start of the recording process. The original line-up that included Craig Hooper evolved into the three-piece of Finn, Hester and Seymour that became associated with the initial period of the band. Hooper went back to his old band, The Reels, after realising things were not working out. The plan was to recruit a replacement, but something clicked with the three-piece that remained. Bassist Nick Seymour has said that there was an '... instinctive, intuitive chemistry between us from day one'.[4]

The band set off for Los Angeles in the summer of 1985, trying to secure a record deal with the demos they had put together. Capitol Records was the desired label, given Finn's love for The Beatles.

When they secured a deal, it was signed with two stipulations. One was a change of name; the label was not convinced by The Mullanes as a band name. It sounded too much like an Irish folk band for their liking. The label was pushing for something along the lines of 'Neil Finn and the...'.

They even went to the local library to find a solution. Looking through books at random, Neil came across a phrase which was initially suitable for the album's title. But their ideas for a band name just made Capitol choke. Largest Living Things was the leading candidate; others included Krakatoa Chorus, Barbara Stanwyck's Chest and even the Record Company. There was a lot of indecision, and it was just before the deadline for the cover art that they took the easy option. 'Crowded House sounded strange to a lot of people, but so does every band name when you first hear it,' says Stamler. 'It certainly fitted!'[5]

Crowded House was also an apt description of their living conditions in the Sycamore Avenue home in LA during the recording process. A small dwelling that became party central for the Australian diaspora in LA.

The other requirement was that they should work with Mitchell Froom. Tom Whalley was looking for the right producer for the band. Froom was also starting his career as a producer, and he was chosen despite having only a few credits to his name at that point. In hindsight, this was a fortuitous intervention. Froom has played a vital part throughout the Crowded House story and still does to this day.

His production work has stood the test of time; there are a lot of albums from that period that have dated very badly. Froom's production is the perfect counterpoint to the songs that Finn had written. He subtly layered them with keyboards, layered guitars and Stax-esque horn bursts, bringing a soulfulness to some of the arrangements. This separates it from many of the albums released at the time, giving it a more organic sound.

Given that the funding was coming from the American label, the album was resolutely aimed at the US market. The esoteric sound of Split Enz gave way to a more eclectic classic pop.

The debut album would also mark the start of a tradition in the band of bassist Nick Seymour designing the album artwork. Though it took some time convincing his bandmates and the record label, it was a dream come true when he got his wish. The picture was based on his inspiration from British-born New York-based expressionist Sue Coe and the Mexican painter Frida Kahlo. Neil Finn was in his favourite colour; red. Nick Seymour was on a Naples Yellow podium holding a cut-down bass. Drummer Paul Hester, who was fond of his nap time, is seen astral-travelling in pyjama bottoms blown through the proscenium arch by a desktop fan. Seymour recounted his inspiration for the cover on the deluxe edition, saying of his representation of Hester: 'I have been often asked why I depicted Paul as an Angelic spectral-like presence. I never for one minute entertained the thought of not growing old gracefully with him.'[6]

The eponymous debut album was released in June 1986. It was a slow process for the album to receive the acclaim it now has today. A deluxe edition was released in November 2016, which includes an assortment of demos and songs that missed the cut for the original album release.

The tracks

'Mean To Me'

Written by Neil Finn
Duration: 3:17
Released as a single in June 1986

The band's first single was only given an Australian release. It gave fans of Split Enz a taste of what was to come from the band. There is a strummed first verse that sets the scene of the song. The chorus explodes into life and has that mixture of sprightly music with quirky lyrics that would become the band's trademark for the next few albums. It is a brisk number with an impassioned vocal from Neil Finn.

Two separate songs have been joined together to make this one. In its finished version, there is certainly no knowing that. It all sounds so seamless. The lyrics stem from a real-life encounter with a superfan of Split Enz who wrote a letter to Finn asking if they could meet up. They did, and Neil Finn told the *NZ Herald* in 2001 the story of that encounter:

> I met her and had ten minutes with her. Then I came back later, and she was dancing with Gary McCormick, so I wrote those lines in which I did intimate they'd got it on. She bailed me up in LA about three years later and was most upset. She swears she didn't. I felt chastened by that.[7]

'World Where You Live'

Written by Neil Finn
Duration: 3:05
Released as a single in July 1986

Technically, the band's second single, but it was the first to be released beyond their home territory. It is another one that has an intriguing origin, also inspired by real events. When recording the album in LA, Neil Finn would stay at his manager's apartment. Prompted by hearing his neighbour having sex, he wrote the song inspired by the strange noises he was hearing:

> The 'Here's someone now who's got the muscle' was that guy. And then, 'I don't know where you go, do you climb into space'—they were sort of mysterious sounds, so that was me thinking about what people would get up to.[8]

The harmonies in the chorus elevate the song. The verses have staccato guitars underpinned by a great bassline that drives the song. It is typical of the white-funk basslines of the day. The coda is marvellous too; it is often elongated to good effect when the song is played live. It has been an ever-present in the setlist since the day it was released.

Two songs into the album, and both strong singles that pointed the way the band would evolve.

'Now We're Getting Somewhere'

Written by Neil Finn
Duration: 4:05
Released as a single in September 1986

Given that Crowded House as a unit was still settling down. It was felt that the rhythm section had not gelled sufficiently to get the definitive recording of this track. There was an impatience on behalf of the label to get this one right, given that it had been earmarked as a potential single. The song has a shuffle beat, and it was felt that the initial recordings were not coming together quickly enough.

That is why Jim Keltner, drums and Jerry Scheff, bass, were drafted in to get this one down. They are renowned session men with a lengthy string of credits to their name. Keltner had played previously with the likes of George Harrison, John Lennon and Ringo Starr. Scheff had Elvis Presley and The Doors as notable lines on his CV. Seymour and Hester initially felt a bit put out by this move, but stepped back for the sake of the song, although they did bond with the hired hands in the studio during the recording and learned a lot from working with them.

It is a jaunty number with the rhythm track at the forefront of the song. If you have hired LA's finest session men, well, you are not going to hide them in the mix. There is a Celtic feel to the song, accentuated by the harmonium. It is another song that had its origins in another demo, 'Stranger Underneath Your Skin'.

Neil Finn has reflected on the song's transformation on his website:

> Mitchell liked the chorus and didn't really like the verse of the original song so we started looking for another verse. Just another example of things that go through quite a major transformation.[9]

It is ironic, given the issues with recording this song, that the shuffle, almost in a busking-style, became a feature of live performances in the band's first incarnation. It is the only single that did not appear on the band's greatest hits collection, *Recurring Dream*.

'Don't Dream It's Over'

Written by Neil Finn
Duration: 3:57
Released as a single in October 1986

It was one of the first songs written for the album and was one of the tracks on the demo tape that got the band signed.

It has done well over the years, if that is not an understatement, but its success was something of a slow build. It was dismissed initially by the UK label as being too 'Beatlesy'. This may have been one of the reasons for the song not doing as well in the UK as it did in other territories. It did well in the US, and that shows that when a label is behind a song, then it has every chance of being a success. Although the push came from the dedication of a record-label staff member and fan:

> There was a woman at Capitol called Paulette McCubbin, who was a junior promotion staff person, but she absolutely adored the record. And she made it her mission to ring all the stations, you know, in smaller markets, and hounded them to play the song. And that's where our initial success came: through secondary markets, and started to perform really well.[10]

The song originated from Neil Finn feeling a bit antisocial while at his brother Tim's house. Neil took himself off into the backroom to play the piano while the guests were next door. It was there that the song came to him. He claimed that 'It was one of those songs that came largely in one go, which doesn't happen very often, and is usually a good sign.'[11]

Bands would kill for a song of the quality and depth of 'Don't Dream It's Over'. From the opening strummed guitar to Seymour's bassline run, it makes the listener sit up and take notice. It contained the distinctive strumming pattern that Seymour has christened the 'Kiwi Party Strum', familiar to many a family gathering in New Zealand.

Then there is the Mitchell Froom solo in the middle that adds a nice Hammond organ part and evokes Procol Harum's Whiter Shade of Pale, giving the song the same timeless feel. It might have been seen as retro at the time, but it is now seen as classic.

Neil and Froom spent three days together working on the songs, the latter expanding on the former's ideas. He suggested a more soulful feel for 'Don't Dream It's Over', came up with a bass part and the organ solo. Neil thought, 'This is great, it's happening.' Froom's minimalist keyboard style was refreshing after the flamboyant verbosity from Eddie Rayner in the Enz.[12]

It is a song that has been covered by numerous acts over the years. It is arguably the band's finest moment. Other songs have got close, more on them later.

On hearing it in the studio one day, Jimmy Iovine, the great U2 producer, heard the record and said it was a classic in a similar vein to that of Lennon and McCartney. A ringing endorsement if ever there was one. A review in *Spin*, by Brian Cullman, talking about the album, singled out the song for praise: He claimed it was 'a sister song to John Lennon's "Watching the Wheels"'.[13]

It seems to be one of those songs that exists beyond the band. During Neil Finn's stint with Fleetwood Mac, it was a song which they covered regularly. Neil Finn talked about other versions on the *Song Exploder Podcast*:

> Ariana Grande sang it in Manchester when they were mourning the loss of a whole lot of people at one of her concerts. And Bono and Edge just performed it in Las Vegas recently as a response to world events, and to the loss of Alexei Navalny. And it continually surprises me where it turns up, and who finds their way into singing it, you know?[14]

In 2025, at the Spark Arena in Auckland, Neil Finn got to perform the song live with Dua Lipa when her massive world tour landed in New Zealand.

Having had time to reflect on the success of the song, when speaking about it on the documentary *Great Australian Albums* in 2007, Neil Finn did say that he had a form of guilt about its massive success. He questioned why it had not happened during his time in Split Enz.

'Love You 'Til The Day I Die'

Written by Neil Finn
Duration: 3:33

It is a song that stems from the early gigs by The Mullanes, with some of the rhythmic elements coming from an even earlier source. It sounds like a distant cousin of the Split Enz song 'Dirty Creature'. The band then had Craig Hooper on guitar, and the heaviness of the song can be attributed to him. It is the most raucous cut on the album.

On his website, Neil Finn comments on the riff-heavy nature of the song and where it came from:

> We discovered a guitar riff at rehearsal on the Mullanes tour with Craig Hooper, who was with us at the time. Two guitars going donk-donk, dangaranga, donk-donk... and that was the origin of the heaviness.[15]

You would not have thought a song written on the mandolin could have ended up this way. A radically different demo version to the album track can be heard on the deluxe edition. There are heartfelt vocals from Neil Finn competing with the full-on mix and arrangement of the song. Add in the crunchy bassline from Nick Seymour, and you get another shade to the rich textures of the album.

'Something So Strong'

Written by Neil Finn and Mitchell Froom
Duration: 2:52
Released as a single in April 1987

Another song that has become something of a perennial on the band's setlists down the years, it is a favourite of most fans. Mitchell Froom gets a co-write for this one and rightly so, given his contributions.

Having heard the original demo, Mitchell Froom took apart the song and rejigged the chorus. The keyboard became the main part of the song. The collaboration was something that Neil Finn welcomed:

> If somebody's got a better idea, you've got to stay open to it. I've seen it happen so many times that something turns into a much better song as a result of abandoning or jettisoning something you've spent a lot of time on. It's liberating to get rid of things that you've slaved over. [16]

It is another song that was written on the mandolin. The demo can be heard on the deluxe edition of the album. The original demo version has been described by the band as a bit 'Greensleevey'. The singalong qualities have been brought to the fore with the version that Mitchell Froom reassembled. Maybe today its production has dated a little; the definitive version of this can be heard on live albums periodically released by the band.

The video for the single starts with a distant band playing the riff to 'Smoke on the Water', before the camera pans to Crowded House playing in a barn, a classic American car parked outside. Even without this, you can see that this one is aimed at the American market. Reminiscing about the band's evolution on the *Farewell to the World* DVD documentary extras, Nick Seymour said that his performance in this video is one of the most cringeworthy moments of his career.

On an album that contains 'Don't Dream It's Over', this has to take second billing on the album, but what a song.

'Hole In the River'

Written by Neil Finn and Eddie Rayner
Duration: 4:00

There is a Doors-y quality to the bassline and the keyboards at the start. The tone of the song sets the mood quite well. Lyrically, this tumbled out of Neil following the suicide of his father's sister. The song's title is from a line from the 1963 movie *Irma La Douce*, in which Shirley MacLaine's character threatens to throw herself off a bridge, 'and make a hole in the river.' The day after seeing the film, Neil was notified of the suicide of his aunt.

There is a discordant outro that fits the song's dark subject matter. It also crops up in the middle eight, too. This sounds like a carryover from the original demo, which was more up-tempo. The chorus/hook is performed in something akin to a rap-style. That element which was written and performed by Paul Hester was left off the final version. The demo version also has differing lyrics. This version can be heard on the 2016 deluxe edition. The slowed-down final and more recognisable version is probably more in keeping with the lyrical tone of the song.

It is a poignant song and one that highlights the variation on the album. The original demo was from the last days of Split Enz, which explains the Eddie Rayner co-write.

'Can't Carry On'

Written by Neil Finn
Duration: 3:57

This is the only track on the album that was not recorded at the studios used in LA. Eddie Rayner and Neil Finn produced this at Platinum Studios, Melbourne.

It is a mid-tempo rocker that earns its place on the album for an eminently hummable chorus. The harmonies are rammed up to the fore. The organ is competing with the AM radio guitars.

Following on from 'Hole in the River', it could be another song of suicidal ideation. Lyrically, it seems to be more about a love gone wrong.

'I Walk Away'

Written by Neil Finn
Duration: 3:07

It is a song that originates from another demo for a potential Split Enz song. It has its origins in the song 'Love & Success'.

Some have also speculated that it could be about a relationship, in particular, the one between Neil and his brother Tim. In truth, it was more about Neil Finn's thoughts on the demise of Split Enz. The chugging guitars at the start sound like it could be the start of a Billy Bragg number, before it settles down into something that is more in keeping with their sound. It builds into another big, typical Crowded House chorus.

'Tombstone'

Written by Neil Finn
Duration: 3:30

'Tombstone' was originally called 'Roll Back the Ocean'. Tim Finn suggested the new title while the brothers Finn holidayed in Italy.

Neil Finn let slip on an episode of his lockdown podcast *Fangradio* in 2020 that it was not one of his favourite songs. It is very rarely you get a Crowded House-by-numbers type of song. This feels like it has the stamp of a classic song, but it fades away in comparison to the rest of the album.

A filler for an album of strong numbers.

'That's What I Call Love'

Written by Paul Hester and Neil Finn
Duration: 3:39

Some of the demos for the album had been done before the line-up had settled down. Nick Seymour had come along and tried out on a few of the numbers. This was the one that got him the gig in the band. It convinced Neil Finn (and his wife Sharon) that he should become a permanent member of the band.

Neil Finn explained: 'Nick performed very well on Paul's song, 'That's What I Call Love,' and that was kind of the clincher. He had a funky bassline. Sharon loved it, and that was when he got the job.'[17]

Nick Seymour certainly deserves the gig on the strength of his performance on this song. He claimed that the inspiration for the bassline came from Chic's bassist Bernard Edwards.

It is a funky song that was typical of the era. There is a bit of Wham in the mix too, especially with the horn stabs. The funky guitars have a touch of 'Chant No. 1 (I Don't Need This Pressure On)' by Spandau Ballet about them as well.

The song got two extra outings on the B-side of 'World Where You Live' and 'Don't Dream It's Over' singles. A funky end to a debut album that promised so much for the future.

B-sides and various other tracks

The songs that appeared on the two singles from this era were also taken from the album. Although there is an extended mix of 'Don't Dream It's Over' on the twelve-inch of 'World Where You Live'. That version extends the song by a couple of minutes. It accentuates the 'Kiwi-strumming style' guitars and pushes the ethereal-sounding keyboards to the fore.

2016 Deluxe Edition bonus disc (Capitol/Universal)

Contains several demos and early/different versions of songs. Some songs that got away but were released eventually. There are two live songs 'Left Hand(live)' and 'Grabbing by the Handful (live)'. These are songs from the short-lived incarnation of the band as The Mullanes. A version of 'Left Hand' has been released elsewhere on the *Afterglow* extras collection.

Tracklist

'Something So Strong' (home demo), 'Hole In The River' (studio demo), 'Love You 'Til The Day I Die' (home demo), 'That's What I Call Love' (studio demo), 'Can't Carry On' (studio demo), 'Walking On The Pier'(studio demo), 'Does Anyone Here, Understand My Girlfriend' (studio demo), 'Oblivion' (studio demo), 'Walking On The Spot'(studio demo), 'Something So Strong'(studio demo), 'Now We're Getting Somewhere' (studio demo), 'Stranger Underneath Your Skin'(home demo), 'Don't Dream It's Over'(home demo), 'Left Hand'(live), 'Grabbing By The Handful'(live), 'World Where You Live'(writing demo), and 'Recurring Dream'(original version).

2

Temple of Low Men (1988)

Original album release:	July 1988
Deluxe Edition release:	November 2016
Personnel:	Neil Finn: guitar, piano and lead vocals Paul Hester: drums and backing vocals Nick Seymour: bass guitar Tim Finn: backing vocals Mitchell Froom: keyboards Richard Thompson: guitar solo on 'Sister Madly' Alex Acuna: percussion Heart Attack Horns: horns
Duration:	38:04
Recorded at:	Capitol Recording Studios, Los Angeles and Sunset Sound Factory, Los Angeles, and Platinum Studios, Melbourne
Produced by:	Mitchell Froom
Recorded by:	Tchad Blake at Platinum Studio, Melbourne, and Sunset Sound Factory, Los Angeles
Chart positions:	Australia: 1; New Zealand: 2; UK: 99; US: 40

Thoughts had already turned to the next album even before 'Something So Strong' was released as the last single from the debut album. Difficult second album syndrome was not seemingly an issue, as Neil Finn had written several new songs ready to record. These were written while on the road and included songs such as 'Sister Madly', 'Mansion in the Slums', 'Never Be the Same' and 'Better Be Home Soon'.

After the slow burn to reach their audience with their debut album, it was time for the band to start recording album number two. In contention for the album title was the self-deprecating *Mediocre Follow-Up*. This was rejected; it was a good job, as the album is anything but that. Even though it is darker and moodier than its predecessor, it was still full of the melodies that would become a trademark of the band. It is an album that contains songs that the band still perform live.

The album was eventually called *Temple of Low Men*. The title was inspired by an extract from *The Book of Euphemism*, a book that producer Tchad Blake had lying around in the studio. Without being too explicit, the title is something that relates to the female anatomy.

Mitchell Froom was again in the production seat, as well as behind the keyboards. His Hammond organ can be heard to good effect on 'Better Be Home Soon', one of the standout songs from the album. The producer's recollection of the recording process was that it was easier to record than their debut. He said:

> It was a painless record to make. People have the idea that the second record was misery and the first was joy. The first was hell, and the second was joy. With the first, we were trying to work out what the band should sound like. More electronic? Did they want to be a band, like Talking Heads? Or like the Pet Shop Boys? How to approach it? But now, they were truly a band—and they were on peak form. Neil had found his voice.[1]

The album was recorded by Tchad Blake at Platinum Studio, Melbourne, and Sunset Sound Factory, Los Angeles. The original album was released in July 1988, nearly two years after their debut.

The album was a critical success in most publications, but there was one notable exception. They received a lukewarm review from the renowned US writer Robert Christgau in his *Consumer Guide*.[2] This clearly stuck with Neil Finn, given that he jokingly referred to the comments at several points throughout his *Fangradio* sessions in 2020/21.

The main issue was that the album did not expand the band's fan base. The die-hard fans from the Split Enz era and new followers who enjoyed the debut Crowded House album went out and bought the album. Other issues that hampered the progress included the record label's reluctance to get behind the album as strongly as they did with the first one. There was the issue of the UK's indifference to all things Crowded House at that time.

In some quarters, it was felt that the album lacked the big hit that 'Don't Dream It's Over' had become. 'Better Be Home Soon' was one of the few tracks seen to have single potential, but when it was released, it did not catch fire as expected. They would eventually release five songs from the album, but all with diminishing returns. A prospective three-month US tour was cancelled as a result, and after a short but successful tour of Canada and Australasia, the band went on indefinite hiatus.

The artwork for the album was again Nick Seymour's creation; he explained his inspirations in sleeve notes for the Deluxe Edition in 2016:

> The cover is oil on card assemblage. The portraits have me sporting a jacket of buildings, Paul's 'upside down' contrariness laid bare by his ever-increasing mood swings and Neil resplendent in his ultimate destination of New Zealand green hills.[3]

A deluxe edition was released on 4 November 2016 and contains several demo and live versions of the songs that appeared on the original album (as well as on future albums).

The tracks

'I Feel Possessed'

Written by Neil Finn
Duration: 3:48
Released as a single in January 1990

Its haunting opening has a film score quality to it. The bass ramps up the song's film noir charm. The keyboards underpin the song quite effectively. They are quite understated, that is until Mitchell Froom is let loose at the end of the song with one of his characteristic Hammond organ swirls. It has got one of those Crowded House choruses that creeps up on you and will have you humming along with.

The lyrics heighten the filmic quality with the use of metaphorical allusions. The possession that the song talks about is that of a relationship, but with more positive connotations. It sets the scene quite well for what follows with the rest of the album.

It was released as the fifth single from the album in Australia in 1990. Something to tide fans over until the band's third album would be released. To keep the completists happy, some of the releases came with live performances by ByrdHouse— a short-lived union featuring Roger McGuinn of The Byrds and Crowded House. The tracks were recorded at the Pantages Theatre, Los Angeles, on 7 April 1989.

'Kill Eye'

Written by Neil Finn
Duration: 3:14

This sounds like a loose number and one that has always gone down well when it gets played live. There have been some great live versions released over the years, notably on the second disc of *Recurring Dream: The Very Best of Crowded House*, which shows off the song as it was intended. The version on the album is a good attempt at getting that live sound down on record. The band was quite tight at the point in time they recorded their second album, and that can be heard on this track. It's one that Neil Finn has enjoyed playing live down the years.

'Kill Eye was always a good jam when we played it with the band. The lyrics are a direct result of watching the news on TV—one too many times.'[4]

The whispered sample at the start, 'I beg you, forgive me', is from the US TV evangelist Jimmy Swaggart's televised apology in May 1988 for his moral transgressions.

There are some screeching sounds at the end that may come from Nick Seymour taking Tchad Blake out to Melbourne to capture some bird song. They could not get an isolated sound, given that it is such a built-up area.

As well as the various live versions, the studio version also appeared on the flip side of the 'Better Be Home' single.

'Into Temptation'

Written by Neil Finn
Duration: 4:34

It has got that great shuffling beat that the band do well. There is a sparseness to the arrangement that almost feels like the song is delivered in hushed tones. When the song does build to the middle eight, it still feels restrained. This is another beautiful arrangement, with great production that does not sound dated when listening to it nearly forty years after its release.

The inspiration for the lyrics came when the ever-observant Neil Finn was touring, and he noticed a rugby team with players going in and out of various rooms at the hotel where he was staying. 'The guilty get no sleep' line is quite telling of the situation he witnessed. The song has other allusions to the infidelities that he observed.

Speaking about the song in 1988, Finn said:

> There are a lot of songs about these days that deal with sex and sexuality in quite a flippant and go-for-it kind of way, which is fine. Prince does it very well in a very uninhibited manner. But you see, I'm from a fairly conservative middle-class, Catholic background, so for me, I can't separate sex from the guilt and faithfulness and all that, and I think that's very much part of it. So, it's written not about myself but about a state of mind that I'm familiar with.[5]

It highlights the step up in the quality of the songwriting from the last album. It is doing the song a disservice calling it a pop song. It is more than that.

The deluxe edition (2016) again gives a good insight into Neil Finn's songwriting process, with several tracks that went into the finished version of 'Into Temptation'. Elements such as 'Dream On' (home demo), 'Never Been Born' (rehearsal), and 'Think I'm Gonna Change' (home demo).

'Mansion In the Slums'

Written by Neil Finn
Duration: 3:46

The first line of the song came to Finn while recording the first album. The incongruously parked caravan that he observed in the leafy hills of LA gave the song its impetus.

It opens in a similar vein to 'Kill Eye', with a heavily strummed guitar line setting the tone before the rest of the band comes in as the arrangement expands. It is said that Finn that the music for the song is inspired by the rhythm of a walk. Talking about the song on his *Fangradio* show, he felt that the song might be a bit too elaborate, but it had some good parts.

Amongst the abstract lyrics, there are some insights into the newfound fame that the band had experienced since the success of their debut album.
'Later on, as we were getting successful, the line resonated for me as I was contemplating what success means, and that sparked a lot of the other lines in the song', Neil Finn, recounted to performing-musician.com in November 2019.[6]

The caravan is referenced on the album cover. Nick Seymour's design managed to weave a picture of it onto the green suit that Neil Finn was wearing. It was almost a case of life imitating art, when the band replicated the design for a stage outfit for Finn to wear during the tours promoting the album. The green baize material they used for the outfit wasn't the best choice as it was too heavy and sweat-inducing for the rigours of a Crowded House live show.

The song gets an additional outing as the B-side of 'Sister Madly', the band's fourth single.

'When You Come'

Written by Neil Finn
Duration: 4:46
Released as a single in August 1988

When you have a song released on a euphemistically titled album, in the age of Prince and Frankie Goes to Hollywood, it is no wonder that people came up with their own meanings as to what 'When You Come' is all about. This is something that Neil Finn has noted down the years, while also suggesting other inspirations:

> I would be naive to think that people would not read erotic imagery into the lyrics! I am conscious of that, but 'When You Come' also has an element of cosmic events, the birth of star systems, and great natural occurrences. I was trying to tie those thoughts together. It is not just about your girlfriend having an orgasm![7]

The lyrics came first and were written almost as a stream of consciousness; the music came later. The middle eight is one of the finest that Finn has written. There is a lightly plucked guitar that sounds like it might be a mandolin. There is a sound of REM at their finest here. It is another of the band's big numbers and inevitably gets performed live to this day. There is a slow build that explodes with the chorus talking about burning and exploding. It does the same musically and metaphorically. Live versions of the song are often just as incendiary. On the record, it gives it a good go. If it is not the best song on the album, then it is not far from being so.

The third single from the album. It also had repeat outings backing several Crowded House singles down the years, and even on solo live releases from Neil Finn.

'Never Be the Same'

Written by Neil Finn
Duration: 4:29

It was never released as a single, but the song did chart in the US mainly due to radio play. It sounds quite upbeat in spirit. It is not one of the songs that stand out on the record. For Neil Finn, his intentions for the song may not have been fully realised with the release. 'My feeling about that song is that there was something slightly not quite right about it. It had a blemish, and I don't know why, but it had more potential.'[8]

There is a line about friends at the funeral that suggests the song is more contemplative and about someone fulfilling their potential. It is listenable, but maybe acts as a comedown song after the highs of the previous number.

'Love This Life'

Written by Neil Finn
Duration: 3:37
Released as a single in August 1988

It is another song that bears the influence of Mitchell Froom. The song was too upbeat for the producer's liking, he compelled Neil Finn to give the song more of a twist with the lyrics, which he did. Finn was in an agreement with the call from Froom:

> At the end of 'Love This Life', I had originally written 'Love them even if they hate you' as a line. It's quite a noble sort of thought. Doesn't matter what they think of you; turn the other cheek. Mitchell suggested changing it to 'even if you think that I hate you,' which is very bitter. It's like you just set up this whole song, and then all of a sudden, it's got a twist. It's like maybe I'm contemptuous of everybody. I allowed him to talk me into it.[9]

Despite the twist, there are some good warnings about not wasting time. The 'pedal my faith' line could be another allusion to the American TV evangelists they would have been exposed to while recording the album in the US.

Musically, the arpeggiated guitar that runs throughout the song acts as the hook. The rhythm section is low in the mix, but their contributions help to give the song that mysterious feel.

'Sister Madly'

Written by Neil Finn
Duration: 2:52
Released as a single in August 1988 (UK), January 1989 (New Zealand), April 1989 (Australia)

The subject of the song is Neil's sister, Judy, who would often wake in the night having anxiety dreams about her school exams. She would wake the house up with her screaming. The 'you're systematically stepping on my head' is a reference to the pair sharing a room when they were younger. She would step over him to get out of the room. In response, she has said that Neil talked in his sleep.

It's another Crowded House song with a shuffle beat, a style that they became more adept at with each passing album. The busking style they adopted during their live formative years served them well. It was a song that Paul Hester would often step to the front of the stage and deliver behind a stand-up drum, playing the brushes. Live, this style showcased the comedic as well as musical talents of the band. Nick Seymour's walking bassline is probably one of the best of his career to date.

There is a great jazz-like guitar solo, performed expertly by Richard Thompson. He is said to have delivered this almost as a first take.

This is a great song. Quite out of step with the sounds of the day, but one that sounds like a classically timeless tune. It was recorded using vintage microphones and amps to get that authentic vintage sound, which it has done so well.

'In The Lowlands'

Written by Neil Finn
Duration: 3:58

The title of the song was again derived from the same source as the album title. It originally started life in another form, which can be heard on the 2016 deluxe edition of *Temple of Low Men* titled 'Fire Will Keep Me Warm (In the Lowlands Home Demo)'

It was recorded during the lead-up to the debut album but was kept back for this album. The song was written in a place that had been quite productive for Finn over the years: 'There were lots of songs written on the piano around that time at Osborne Street. And a guitar and two babies were conceived. It was a fertile house.'[10]

It is not a song that Mitchell Froom particularly liked, as Neil Finn noted on one of his *Fangradio* sessions. It is one where Finn stood his ground and managed to get it on the album. It has all the hallmarks of a catchy Crowded House number. A singable chorus with enough musical hooks to keep the listener interested. There is a great guitar riff in the instrumental section. Despite Froom's misgivings about the song, he delivers the memorable keyboard line running throughout the song, and that builds in the chorus. It also occurs during the instrumental break to good effect.

'Better Be Home Soon'

Written by Neil Finn
Duration: 3:08
Released as a single in June 1988

The song that has sent many a Crowded House fan home happy after they have had the pleasure of seeing the band live. A staple of the band's live set ever since its release. It is a great closer for any live gig, and it is the perfect final number for this album.

It was selected as the lead single from the album. The record label hoped that the record would have a similar impact as 'Don't Dream It's Over' had in terms of sales. It was highly rated by the critics, but it did not bring in the expected numbers. It did well back home in Australia and New Zealand, reaching number two in both countries. It even scored a number one in Canada. In the US, it performed poorly. This was the point at which the band's label, Capitol, stopped promoting the album as extensively as they had planned:

> There was a lot of anticipation for that song. The record company really wanted to go for those 100 miles an hour type hits [as the first single], so we let them. In one way, it's kind of strange because it's not that representative of the rest of the record. The good thing about it—it shows us that more than any other song, probably—is that it's the song in a Crowded House set that people can sing from beginning to end very easily, in a group context, community singing and all that. That's always been a pretty important thing for us.[11]

In a 2021 interview with Apple Music, Neil Finn commented on the song:

> I'm quite happy to have songs that are open-ended enough to lend themselves to any occasion. And that song has indeed been embraced by homesick people, by people who have separated from their loved ones, and by people who have just fallen in love. There's something about the fact that it's a little open-ended that enables that song.[12]

In 2005, not long after the death of drummer Paul Hester, a clearly emotional Neil Finn performed the song solo at the ARIA Awards. The members of APRA

(Australasian Performing Right Association) voted it as the thirty-third best New Zealand song of the twentieth century.

2016 Deluxe Edition bonus disc (Capitol / Universal)

The deluxe edition contains the usual assortment of demos and live tracks. Some songs would appear in updated form on future albums. A notable presence on some of the live tracks is Roger McGuinn from The Byrds. A number of these live tracks had previously appeared as B-sides on singles from the *Woodface* era.

Tracklist

'Whispers and Moans' (home demo), 'Never Be The Same'(home demo), 'Dream On' (home demo), 'Never Been Born'(rehearsal), 'Think I'm Gonna Change'(home demo), 'Into Temptation'(home demo), 'Fire Will Keep Me Warm'(In The Lowlands home demo), 'Love This Life'(home demo),'Sister Madly'(studio out-takes), 'Mansion In The Slums'(live),'This Is Massive'(live), 'Love This Life'(live),'In The Lowlands'(live),'I Feel Possessed'(live),'Burnt Out Tree'(live),'Mr Tambourine Man'(live),'Eight Miles High'(live),'So You Want To Be A Rock'n'roll Star'(live), 'When You Come'(live), 'Sister Madly'(live), 'Better Be Home Soon' (live).

3

Woodface (1991)

Original album release:	June 1991
Deluxe Edition release:	October 2016
Personnel:	Neil Finn: guitars, vocals and keyboards Tim Finn: piano, guitar and vocals Nick Seymour: bass and vocals Paul Hester: drums, vocals, keyboards and percussion Mitchell Froom, Mark Hart and Stuart Ellison: keyboards Alex Acuna: percussion Geoffrey Hales: percussion Jack Mack: brass Ricki Fataar: drums and percussion Peter Bucknell:violin Vince Parsonage: violins David Hidalgo: accordion Geoffrey Hales: percussion Jorge Callendrelli: strings Sharon Finn: backing vocals Chris Wilson: harmonica
Duration:	48:11
Recorded at:	Capitol Recording Studios, Los Angeles and Sunset Sound Factory, Los Angeles, and Platinum Studios, Melbourne
Produced by:	Mitchell Froom and Neil Finn
Chart positions:	Australia: 2; New Zealand: 1; US: 82; UK: 6

Touring commitments for the previous album continued through to 1989, with the band's itinerary seeing them play territories like Japan for the first time. Neil Finn even found time to fit in a Split Enz live reunion at the end of the decade. The brothers Finn also did some live gigs together in the early 90s.

The process of writing and recording the third album was not a straightforward one. Creatively and critically, the second album was perceived to be stronger than their eponymous debut. *Temple of Low Men* had done well in Australia and New Zealand, but they had not matched the sales of the first album in the US. It was deemed to be lacking 'the killer song'; commercially, *Temple of Low Men* suffered death by a thousand shrugs. 'It underperformed everywhere and Neil was very upset', the band's former co-manager Gary Stamler said reflecting on the performance of the second album.[1]

They still had champions at Capitol Records, but the label wanted to see a better return on their investment. They wanted sales matching those of the first album. The record company had a new president, Hale Milgram, who made it his mission to improve sales. He was willing to invest money in the next album, which came in the form of increased promotion and slicker videos.

One thing they could not replicate was the relative ease that came with writing and recording the first two albums. In truth, the band was a little burned out. Neil Finn was struggling to repeat the formula of before. He had an initial batch of twelve songs, but only six were deemed suitable for the next album.

Capitol rejected the band's first take of the new record. Although it included immaculate cuts such as 'Four Seasons in One Day' and 'Fall at Your Feet', Neil knew in his gut that he had not come up with a whole album's worth of brilliant material. The thought of it was making him physically sick, as Dino Scatena noted in the liner notes of the 2016 Deluxe Edition of the album.[2]

There were also tensions within the band. It seemed that Nick Seymour's days were numbered as a member of Crowded House. According to Seymour, when he asked Neil for an explanation, he simply replied: 'You're just not pushing my creative buttons anymore.'[3]

People around Neil Finn questioned whether this was the right decision for the band. Neil questioned his moves in later years:

> I look back…with a little bit of sadness at that, but in a way, it was resolved in such a great way. I still remember the day. I think there were just frustrations growing up there. The idea is that you want people to be like you. You want to remodel them, in your own image, and now I think now in the passage of time, we enjoy each other's differences, and we recognise that's what makes bands great.[4]

Thankfully, Neil Finn changed his mind and was understanding of why he had made that decision in the first place:

> I just didn't find that the bass was doing stuff that I wanted it to. I was playing bass on my own demos and kinda liking what I was doing. It was classic lead-singer syndrome: you want to do everything?[5]

With the impasse with the recording of the Crowded House album, Neil Finn looked to other avenues to overcome the issues 'It was then that his mind flashed back to the KCW radio session back in February 1988, when he and Tim had hinted at a possible Finn Brothers record.'[6] Neil Finn hooked up with his brother to write what would hopefully become the first Finn Brothers album. This was the impetus that he needed after the record label had rejected his first demos. This was something that he had thought about doing for a long time.

The recollection of this session spurred the two brothers to get together to write. The songs they were writing were very harmony-oriented, suited to the brothers singing together. The process of writing with Tim Finn seemed easier than finishing the songs for the new Crowded House album. The brothers were on a rich, creative streak.

There were two albums and two bands on the go at the time. The logic would be to focus on one album, the new Crowded House one. This became apparent to the band, especially Neil Finn. Tim Finn was not going to give up the songs that he had written with his brother that lightly, either. It made sense for Tim to join Crowded House:

> It became very obvious to all of us that the album would be very strong with both Tim and the songs he and I had written, that it would be far less schizophrenic than it was when we were planning two records—a duo record and a Crowded House record. When we were going to release them was becoming a nightmare, so it's been good for everybody.[7]

The eventual recording of what would become *Woodface* was a similar process to previous ones. It took over a year to record. They started the process at A&M studios in LA before decamping to Tim Finn's home studio in Melbourne. They went back to LA to finish off, where they were reunited with producer Mitchell Froom. He had a clear idea of what the band needed to do to complete the third album.

Out of the toil and upheaval came the band's most successful album to date. The album was released in June 1991. If *Woodface* sealed the end of mainstream America's interest in Crowded House, the album's fortunes were saved at the eleventh hour by a previously rather indifferent Britain. Released in July 1991, the album looked like it would follow the same sales pattern in the UK as before; that was until 'Weather with You' became a Top 10 hit the following February. This is despite the release of what Froom regards as a 'really awful' radio edit.[8]

There was a change in attitude towards the band in the UK. Their label Parlophone felt that they could get behind the album, especially with singles

'Four Seasons in One Day' and 'Weather with You' ready to roll. The UK music press also changed its outlook towards the band. They had dismissed the first albums as being too AOR, but embraced *Woodface* critically.

UK listeners had, until then, seemed to have only a passing interest in the band. The Crowded House LP had 'peaked' in the UK at number 99; Temple of Low Men had not even made the album chart. And while 'Chocolate Cake' was no smash, only reaching number 69, it was the subsequent releases from Woodface that changed the band's fortunes in the UK.[9]

The UK live dates can be seen as a good barometer of how the UK turned their attention to the band. Crowded House debuted the album live in a promo tour before no more than 300 fans at The Borderline in London on 12 June 1991. Over a year later, on 24 June 1992, they were back playing in London, but now before 10,000 people at Wembley Arena.

Despite the success of the UK tour, tensions surfaced while out on the road between the two brothers. Feeling little kinship to any Crowded House song he had not helped write, Tim Finn spent the majority of each gig standing behind his keyboard, feeling like 'a shag on a rock'. The end came in November 1991, before a show in Glasgow, presaged by what former co-manager Gary Stamler recalls as a '...dark period on the road. I'd get calls from Neil telling me that Tim was appropriating his stage space. There were fights, brotherly snipes, disagreements. A lot of bad karma.'[10]

Tim Finn joining the band did not work out in the live arena. Neil Finn described this as 'trying to put a square peg in a round hole. Tim's a frontman. He always has been and always will be. He deserves to be flailing around and singing, dancing to his heart's content. We stuck him behind a keyboard trying to play keyboardy parts, manipulate buttons and then come down now and again with an acoustic guitar. It interfered with his way of performing and ours, too.'[11]

However, Tim did join Neil at their Wembley Arena gig for 'Weather with You', proving that their bond, both musical and fraternal, was still strong.[12] It was a fitting way to sum up the *Woodface* campaign in the UK. One that brought with it new followers, lots of awards and critical appreciation.

Neil Finn, talking about Woodface on the Great Australian Albums documentary, said that the album is not his favourite and is probably two songs too long, although he does not say which ones in this interview. 'The anomalies in the record put me off it. It does not have a sense of cohesion, but it ended up hanging together.[13]

Again, the cover was a Nick Seymour creation. The design preceded the album. It also inspired its title. There are subtle nods to Split Enz in the costume designs on the back; this was a reflection of the band being unsure about their identity since they had brought Tim Finn into the fold, as Nick Seymour said:

> Simple and bold was the directive. An iconic image that would leap off the CD display rack. I don't remember how I arrived at the facial construct.

> I liked the idea of the band being eyes, nose and mouth. I painted the face and photographed each of the band members in silk robes, then placed them into the facial cavities like a tree house/cubby. The face itself was the obvious hook. Being well aware of my complexities when trying to design, I was delighted when Tim suggested the face on its own... which then made the album naming easy.[14]

The original album was released in June 1991, with the deluxe edition following in October 2016. Several of the Finn Brothers demos from the Murchison St sessions can be found on the deluxe edition. These tracks can be found elsewhere, too. The debut Finn Brothers album, *Finn*, saw an expanded edition lovingly rereleased in 2023 on Pete Paphides' Needle Mythology label. This includes the original eleven-track album, plus the demos for the songs that were intended for the *Finn* album but ultimately appeared on *Woodface*.

The tracks

'Chocolate Cake'

Written by Neil Finn and Tim Finn
Duration: 4:02
Released as a single in May 1991

The album opens with one of the first of the Finn Brothers collaborations. The song came together quite quickly. The song's co-writer, Tim Finn, said that the song's inspiration came from a conversation overheard while the brothers were having dinner in a restaurant: 'I'd heard this woman saying, at the end of a long meal, "I don't know. Should I have another piece of chocolate cake or the cheque?"'[15]

There is a lounge-bar looseness to the arrangement. The piano is the dominant instrument. There are some distinctive percussive sounds throughout. There is some brass, too. It is a mix of genres. There is a bluesy feel to it, something not heard before on a Crowded House number. There is a touch of Eastern music on the fade-out. The harmonies in the breaks are sampled using Neil Finn's Optigan vintage synth. Chris Wilson added the distinctive harmonica, which was captured with the first take. This was despite having heard the track in the studio once. Musically, from the opening rimshot, it marks a typically melodic, jaunty Crowded House number.

It may not be the most conventional first single from a record, but whenever did Crowded House do the obvious? It could be deemed to be a bit of a novelty, not indicative of the rest of the album.

Lyrically, it could be seen as biting the hand that feeds it. The song, with a tongue planted firmly in cheek, is a satire on mass consumption and consumerism, particularly in the US. This could be seen as brave, especially as their US label Capitol had been the band's major benefactor up to that point.

There are several topical and satirical references to add to the mix. Andrew Lloyd Webber gets it in the neck at some point. He gets more of a kicking in the demo version, with a less-than-subtle nod to his show tune 'Don't Cry for Me Argentina'.

The references to cricket may not be understood by a US audience, but there are enough cultural references to keep them happy, or not as the case may be. The US market was unsure about the jokiness of the song. *Rolling Stone* noted reservations about what they perceived as an anti-American message.

Reviewing *Woodface* for *Rolling Stone*, Kristine McKenna questioned the choice of 'Chocolate Cake' as the lead single. 'This song seems hypocritical given that Crowded House relocated to LA to kick its career into high gear,' she wrote. While that was not exactly true—they had worked in the US but had not shifted base from Melbourne—much of the review was full of praise (she described *Woodface* as a 'swinging record and the band as cheerful yet sardonic, sleek, urbane and highly melodic), her comments about 'Chocolate Cake' proved prescient.

While the single charted strongly on Billboard's Alternative Airplay chart, it was not a mainstream hit in America and only managed to reach number 20 in Australia.[16]

'It's Only Natural'

Written by Neil Finn and Tim Finn
Duration: 3:32
Released as a single in December 1991

Another of the collaborative efforts that made the album. It came from a Tim Finn chorus that he had knocking around and Neil had a verse that seemed to go well with it.

It has a very Beatles-ish feel to it, for instance, in the harmonies. This is something that Tim Finn has acknowledged when talking about the album.

There is a quirky, cartoonish opening. There is an understated Nick Seymour bassline buried in the mix, which may have been inspired by 'West End Girls' by the Pet Shop Boys. a song he was listening to on the journey to record the song. A catchy, chiming guitar pattern opens the song and returns throughout the song. The Finn brothers' vocals complement each other quite well. It is an exceptional single. Only Crowded House could use minor chords in the chorus and make that part of the song uplifting.

The title could be seen as a nod to Tim joining the band. Lyrically, though, the inspiration may be something more elemental, as Neil Finn noted in the *Great Australian Album* documentary:

> We wrote the lyrics on the spot. We were talking a lot, at that time, about subatomic particles and quarks. There were two songs around that time - we wrote another one called 'Strangeness and Charm', and they were both named quarks. 'It's Only Natural'—the first verse was very much influenced by that conversation as well. The rubbing together of spirituality and science.[17]

'Fall At Your Feet'

Written by Neil Finn
Duration: 3:19
Released as a single in August 1991

One of the great reasons for purchasing the deluxe editions of the Crowded House albums is to hear how the songs that you know and love have been formulated. 'Fall At Your Feet' is one of those songs that seems to have been finished with as much perspiration as inspiration.

A great deal of time and effort went into getting this song together. How it turned out made it all worth it. It was a solo Neil Finn effort and was written at Osborne St, the ever-fruitful Finn family residence in Melbourne. It had its great chorus for a while, but the verses were not working out as Neil Finn has noted:

> It was a convoluted one, that one. We knew the chorus was really strong. We were lacking a good verse for it, and I happened to be jamming one day with the band in the studio, and we were playing an old piece of mine, which became the verse of that song. Mitchell Froom jumped on it and said, 'That's it', and I finished the lyrics on the spot, and we had it within about two hours. It had a good energy about it.[18]

An early version can be heard on the 2016 deluxe edition; the verse was preserved in some form as 'Left Hand', versions of that song date back to the days of The Mullanes' live gigs. The completed version of 'Left Hand' can be heard on the *Afterglow* album. It highlights that the demo was two songs in need of finding a suitable form. It shows the skills that Mitchell Froom brought to his role as producer.

He spoke to the UK's *The Word* magazine about how it came together:

> I remember listening to the first batch of demos, and there was this piece of music that started nicely, but it was very vague-sounding, very spacey. Then the chorus came in, and it just completely knocked me over. It was so beautiful—the lyric and the melody and the chords were all there, but the rest of the song didn't do that service. I called Neil and said, 'That may be the best thing you have, but you need to raise the bar on the verses. It needs to be more direct.'[19]

The final version sounds like the perfect distillation of what a Crowded House song should be. The song is underpinned by a hooky bassline that delivers the verse to the chorus. The chorus shows that the endeavour of shaping the song was worth it. Musically, it is quite a beautiful, fragile number. There is a piano motif that continues throughout the song to good effect. It is a song that Neil Finn said on his *Fangradio* show, talking about *Woodface,* is up there with his favourite Crowded House numbers. It is also a favourite of former collaborator and friend Richard Thompson.

'Tall Trees'

Written by Neil Finn and Tim Finn
Duration: 2:20

A fairly perfunctory, rockier number that nestles in the running order between the big-hitting singles. It is the song with the shortest run time on the album.

It is an older number that was written about eight to ten years before *Woodface*. The genesis of the song is from an old demo tape that resurfaced and was tidied up for the release of the album. The lyrics are about staying close to your roots. It was another Finn Brothers co-write. It is not a bad song; it just feels a little routine. In an interview in 2024, Neil described the two additional tracks as 'shit' and 'Tall Trees' as a 'low point' on the album.[20]

'Weather With You'

Written by Neil Finn and Tim Finn
Duration: 3:44
Released as a single in February 1992

The fourth single to be released off the album, and what a song it is. It is another one of those songs that is recognisable beyond a fanbase, a song that even if you do not know much about Crowded House, you will know this one. It is the killer hit that all songwriters strive to write. It is the type of song that keeps record labels happy.

This was the first song that Neil and Tim wrote for a mooted Finn brothers' collaboration. Tim Finn had the title and a few lines from the song ready to go. That song came together quite quickly from the moment that Tim Finn sang the line 'walking round the room singing stormy weather'. The tempestuous Melbourne weather may well have been the inspiration for that line.

The original version had differing lyrics on the verse, but the tune and arrangement are very much as they were on the demo. It was a song that came from the first day of writing. The title and the chorus were in place, and the other lyrics came together quickly at the flat on Murchison Street, Melbourne.

Another street is mentioned in the song '57 Mount Pleasant Street'. This is a fictitious address, although it might have been inspired by a similar-sounding address that the Finns' sister lived at in Auckland.

The opening line namechecks 'Stormy Weather'. The song may have come to mind owing to family friend Peggy Dawson, who the brothers remembered as someone who could belt out that song on the piano at their childhood home in Teasdale Street .

Tim Finn recalls how the song emerged.

> We decided to write songs that were very harmony-oriented so that we could sing them together. The songs just flowed, and we recorded them with Paul Hester. Paul played brushes and grooved along on a snare drum.[21]

A great deal of the released version contains elements of what was intended to appear on the planned Finn brothers album. That is why Ricki Fataar (a former member of The Rutles) is credited with playing drums on this track and not Paul Hester. He also contributed to the songs 'All I Ask' and 'There Goes God'. All three were initially destined to be part of that record.

The distinctive riff was recorded on a twelve-string guitar, which gives it that chiming quality. The middle-eight break has a great bassline from Nick Seymour. This is something that the band have fun extemporising and extending live.

The evocative outro (elements also appear in the break) that brings to life the elements in the song stems from a sample of an unknown South African woman playing a jaw-harp. When they toured the country during the *Woodface* era, the copyright holder came forward looking for a cut in the royalties. The band were happy to pay up to the copyright holder, though sadly not directly to the woman herself.

Despite having left the band when it was a hit, Tim Finn was rightly proud of his contributions to the song:

> I remember being back home in Melbourne [having left the band in late 1991] and I received the call that 'Weather with You' was number seven on the UK top ten. I played the song as loud as the studio could take it and just felt the bliss. So, it didn't feel like, oh, I should be there sharing the glory or whatever. It just felt so good to have written a song that could do that, and recording it in my house too.[22]

'Whispers And Moans'

Written by Neil Finn
Duration: 3:40

A song that originates from around the time of the release of the first album. A demo version of early versions of the song appears on the deluxe edition of 'Temple of Low Men'.

Not for the first time, the bass comes to the fore on this one. Cheap Trick were playing in the studio next door and lent Nick their Gecko bass guitar. That is where the double-bass style sound came from.

The song has a slow build and a great lifting chorus. The guitar line has a great hook. There are some great textures present throughout the song. The harmonies are perfect. It sounds quite intricate at times, but the layers are subtly done. Each time you listen to it, something else captures your attention. The instrumental break ramps up the volume, but it complements the verses quite well.

Neil Finn has highlighted the process involved in how the vocals came together for the song:

> There are some quite elaborate backing vocals on that song, which we spent time on. It's interesting that even the songs that Tim wasn't theoretically in the band for, he ended up doing backing vocals on almost all of them before we had incorporated him into the band. This one's a good example. Tim sang backgrounds on the chorus for that.[23]

'Four Seasons in One Day'

Written by Neil Finn and Neil Finn
Duration: 2:50
Released as a single in June 1992

Yet another from the productive Finn Brothers sessions. Percussive brushes are to the fore on this most delicate of songs. The line about 'the black clouds hanging over the domain' springs from the same inspirations as 'Weather with You' and the tempestuous Melbourne weather.

The song could also have other inspirations. The first is the botanical garden in Melbourne called 'The Domain', or it could be a more prosaic reference to the room they wrote the song in.

It could also be about the brotherly relationship that had come together for an album at this time. This is something that Neil Finn alludes to in the *Great Australian Albums* documentary: 'We were both, Tim and I, pretty mercurial and riding emotional rollercoasters all the time. So, it was a good description of the many moods of us collectively and individually.'[24]

The finished version managed to capture the essence of the demo, something that does not always happen. The keyboard part is brought to the fore in the finished version. They managed to retain a great deal of the intimacy of the demo, even with the embellishments. It is hard not to reflect on this song and think of The Beatles. The song distils the essence of their great work into this number. Neil and Tim Finn work similarly; they have always been about great melody and harmonies. It is hard not to make those comparisons with a song like this. The backing crowd harmonies, which were incorporated into the song came from a tape that Tchad Blake had.

Neil Finn noted that the song came from another of their productive writing sessions:

> The music was written first. I spent an afternoon in Melbourne playing a keyboard with string sounds on it, just writing string parts and playing piano parts. The music for both 'Into Temptation' and 'Four Seasons in One Day' happened at the same time. They were part of the same piece at one point, and are sister songs in tempo and atmosphere.[25]

It was the fifth and final song to be released from the album. It charted quite well across the world. The various multiple single releases would have appealed to completists and helped the song attain its healthy chart position.

'There Goes God'

Written by Neil Finn and Neil Finn
Duration: 3:50

It opens with a nice bit of mystical psychedelic guitar and wailing harmonica. Some nonsensical lyrics have an Indian mysticism attached to them. It might be the first time that Crowded House get psychedelic in their career. This one is less influenced by The Beatles and more by those bands that came in the latter part of the 1960s. One such band that may have influenced the song is The Byrds. Their lead singer, Roger McQuinn, was someone the band played with live in 1989, which may have subconsciously influenced the style of this track.

The demo is a straightforward affair. Initially, the song did not have the otherworldly harmonica part, but this was added, not by divine intervention, but another form, as Neil Finn notes on his website:

> It wasn't our initial idea to puta harmonica on the song at all, but Chris Wilson heard us playing in Prahran, and he was very attached to the song and said, 'Let me have a play on it when you come to record it.' So, we got him up, and he crouched down before we were about to start playing the song and looked completely lost and in some private thoughts. Then the song started, and he stood up and raised his arm into the heavens and played one take. We kept the entire take, and we asked him, 'What were you doing, Chris? You know, you looked pretty flamboyant, pretty dramatic,' and he said, 'Oh, I was just pretending I was God.'[26]

Lyrically it is written from the point of view of a child asking a parent about God. Neil Finn revealed on the *Fangradio* show that discussed *Woodface* that his mother was not sure about the song given her staunch Catholicism. As he explained, it was another tongue-in-cheek number. Thankfully, the song was not taken too literally, and they avoided the record-burning that The Beatles suffered at the height of their fame.

'Fame Is'

Written by Neil Finn
Duration: 2:23

This is probably the most up-and-at-'em, rockier songs on the album. Its construction and form sound like something that could have appeared on the band's previous two albums.

There are a lot of spiritual allusions throughout *Woodface*. The lyrical inspiration seems to stem from the band's time working in LA, as well as an old religious order, as Neil Finn notes:

> I was told about this order of religious people in the Middle East, somewhere called the Handmaidens of End Time, and it struck a chord. But I apply it in this song to the new agers, particularly the Californian variety who, under the pretence of being on a quest for spiritual enlightenment, are just trying to be successful and become famous.[27]

'All I Ask'

Written by Neil Finn and Tim Finn
Duration: 3:56

It is another song from the Finn brothers' initial recording sessions, when several good-quality songs seemed to be flowing through the pair. This was one of them. The demo version is sparse and stripped back. That version, which can be heard on the deluxe edition.

Tim Finn sings the lead vocals. Even with the demo version, the harmonies are pinpoint and evocative. The emotional aspect is not lost with the more polished, release.

There was something very filmic about the song. Sounds like something that you could hear on a classic Hollywood soundtrack. You could see a video for this in black and white.

The filmic style was something that Mitchell Froom suggested they try out with the song. It has some lush and beautiful orchestration. It works well as a counterpoint to the other styles on the album.

Neil Finn was pleased with the final results:

> It's unusual because we'd never really had the time or the money available to do strings properly. We were able to get an incredibly good twenty-two piece string section, and so it was just pure delight for us. I was able to sit in the studio and hear a really good string section playing something Tim and I had written together. It knocked us out.[28]

The band wore their best suits during the recording of the song. That was to show the reverence for what they had written and the calibre of extra players they were recording with.

'As Sure as I Am'

Written by Neil Finn
Duration: 2:53

There is an intricacy to it that made it quite hard to play live, which the band rarely did.

Lyrically, it has some weighty concepts, for instance, the extinction of the rhino, but in truth, it is a light-hearted jab at people's apathetic nature. It features a great accordion part from David Hidalgo of Los Lobos. He came on the recommendation of Mitchell Froom, who had previously worked with him.

Neil Finn talking about the intricacies of the song:

> When the idea came up for the accordion, he came down and found it quite difficult because it's not an easy song. But he ended up playing beautifully on it, so it was really great to have. He's a great accordion player, and he's got a fantastic voice too.[29]

The accordion part elevates it from the original demo, which showed that it had potential. There is a tender backing vocal from Neil's wife, Sharon, on the fade out that does not appear on the finished version, unless it is just buried in the mix.

'Italian Plastic'

Written by Paul Hester
Duration: 3:40

This is one of those seemingly throw-away, but ultimately great Paul Hester contributions.

Neil Finn outlined Paul Hester's inspirations for the song:

> It's a Baroque love song, as [Paul] calls it. It's not particularly Italian, but he once bought some really tacky Italian souvenirs for his girlfriend and brought them home, and she found them quite pathetic, I think, so that inspired the song.[30]

It has a great guitar opening, allied to the brilliant Hester lyrics and vocals. It has some great little embellishments. There is a nice bit of melodica in the break. Mark Hart announces his presence in the band with this contribution. The harmonies in the chorus are sublime. The bassline is loose and hooky, just as you would come to expect from Nick Seymour.

There is a nice fade out which threatens to get the hoedown started, with the 'who you gonna take to the ball tonight?' refrain.

Neil Finn felt that the song deserved its place on the album:

> Paul always had good humour in his songs, but I think this is one of his best because it had a very memorable melody and a strong chorus, and it really stuck its head up as fully deserving. It wasn't just a sort of tack-on on this record at all. It deserved to be there. Great lyrics.[31]

There is a demo of this available on the deluxe edition that is worth listening to. This is something that Neil Finn tackles. It lacks the flourishes of the finished version, but it showed its potential even then. The bassline is more dominant and is the leading instrument on that version.

'She Goes On'

Written by Neil Finn
Duration: 3:17

This is the most heartfelt and personal song to appear on the album. It was written for a friend, and Neil Finn played it at their mother's funeral in tribute.

It started life as 'Song for Loma', and it was never the intention for it to be released as a Crowded House song, but it was felt to be one of the strongest songs they recorded while making the album.

Neil Finn has talked about how the meaning of the song has been misconstrued over the years: 'A lot of people think It is a love song, which is great because I wanted it to be the most positive song you could write about something ultimately very black.'[32]

I can see why people have read different meanings into the song. It is a love song, but one that is memorialising a dear departed friend. It is hard not to imagine that many a Crowded House fan has included this song in putting together remembrances of their own loved ones.

A lovely minimalist number, the sparse arrangement fits the mood of the song.

'How Will You Go'

Written by Neil Finn and Tim Finn
Duration: 4:46

The 'final' song of the album, and it is another mellow one to draw the album to a close. It was a song that came from the collaborative approach the Finn brothers employed on many of the songs on the album. Musically, Tim came up with the verse, Neil the chorus and the bridge.

The song was written in tribute to a recording engineer friend of the Finns who had committed suicide. It has a lullaby mantra quality to it. It is a beautifully arranged number. It was the last chance on the album for the Finns to show off their two-part harmonies, which had been used to good effect throughout.

This is something Neil Finn was glad to have the opportunity to do with this album, even with all the issues that came with it:

> Singing with Tim, it was an extreme pleasure, and the most pleasurable aspect of it was that, really, in Split Enz, we never exploited the two-part harmony thing as much as we should have, and we feel with this record we really pulled something out, which we haven't really done since we were boys together performing for our parents' friends.[33]

The loose arrangement with minimalist backing fits in with the mood of the album.

The song fades out at the three-minute mark, and listeners of the CD, will see that there is additional running time…

The unsuspecting listener may be caught unawares with the sounds still emanating from their player when spinning *Woodface* right up to the last bars of the 'final' track, the mellow ending that gave way to this raucous jam.

As was the vogue back in the day, bands liked to hide tracks at the end (in some cases, the pre-gap at the start), making use of the bandwidth of the compact disc. 'I'm Still Here' is the uncredited missing track on the album. On the original CD, the song takes up the remaining 90 seconds of the track. There is a more complete version available on the deluxe box set.

Though Paul Hester counts this in, it might have been Neil Finn playing the drums. It sounds like the verse has lead vocals from Nick Seymour.

'I was lying on the floor on my back, playing guitar, and Neil was playing drums. There were people around I did not even know. It all went down', Paul Hester recounted to Chris Bourke.[34]

It might not have been a classic Crowded House number, but it served a purpose for the band as Mitchell Froom recounted to *The Word* magazine in June 2008:

> We were all getting a little stressed out, and so this idea came up of just having a very free day at the studio. I don't want to get real specific about it, but anyone could show up in any kind of drink or drug state, do whatever they wanted. The day started kind of late and wild and immediately. Everyone got on different instruments. Neil was playing drums a lot, and Paul Hester, had some hysterically funny stream-of-consciousness rants ['I'm Still Here']. It was a tragic musical day, but it was fun. We needed to clear the air.[35]

It did the trick. At the end of the session, Neil Finn pulled out a song that he had written as a 17-year-old, which caught the ear of the producer. That song was 'Fall at Your Feet'.

In a nod to the hidden nature of the song, the information about it is tucked away on Neil Finn's informative website, which offers some great explanations about his craft. In this case, it is tucked away and almost out of view. Keep on scrolling to the bottom of the page (www.neilfinn.com/how-will-you-go) and you will find more information about the song.

2016 Deluxe Edition bonus disc (Capitol/Universal)

The deluxe edition contains the usual assortment of demos and live tracks. Some songs would appear in a more polished form on future albums.

Tracklist

'Burnt Out Tree' (home demo), 'I May Be Late'(home demo), 'She Goes On'(home demo), 'As Sure As I Am'(home demo), 'My Legs Are Gone'(studio demo), 'You Got Me Going'(home demo), 'Italian Plastic'(home demo), 'Be My Guest'(home demo), 'Weather With You'(home demo), 'Chocolate Cake'(home demo), 'How Will You Go'(home demo), 'It's Only Natural' (home demo), 'Four Seasons In One Day'(home demo), 'There Goes God'(home demo), 'Catherine Wheel'(home demo), 'All I Ask'(home demo), 'Fields Are Full Of Your Kind', 'Creek Song/Left Hand', 'Fall At Your Feet' (early version rehearsal), 'The Burglar's Song'(Medley)—Around the UK in 7 Minutes'(live) and 'I'm Still Here'(full version).

4

Together Alone (1993)

Original album release:	October 1993
Deluxe Edition release:	November 2016
Personnel:	Neil Finn: vocals, acoustic and electric guitars, piano and keyboards Nick Seymour: bass, backing vocals and melodica Paul Hester: drums, percussion and vocals Mark Hart: keyboards, electric and acoustic guitars, lap steel guitar and mandolin Eddie Rayner: keyboards on 'Kare Kare' and 'Pineapple Head' Noel Crombie: percussion on 'Private Universe' Geoffrey Hales: percussion on 'Fingers of Love' and 'Locked Out' Tim Finn: backing vocals on 'In My Command' and 'Catherine Wheels' Sharon Finn: backing vocals on 'Black and White Boy', 'Fingers of Love' and 'Private Universe' Dror Erez: accordion on 'Walking on the Spot' Te Waka Huia Cultural Group Choir: vocals on 'Together Alone', 'In My Command' and 'Catherine Wheels' Joe, Tereo, Martie, Jamee, Benjamin: log drummers on 'Together Alone' and 'Private Universe' Clyde Dixon, Stephen Bremner, Laura Astridge, David Bremner, and Shaun Jarrett: brass band on 'In My Command' and 'Together Alone'
Duration:	51:32

Recorded at:	Nigel and Jody Horrocks' House, Karekare; Periscope Studios, Melbourne; Platinum Studios, Melbourne
Produced by:	Youth
Chart positions:	Australia: 2; New Zealand: 1; US: 73; UK: 4

Coming off the back of the *Woodface* tour and album, there was a good momentum going into the recording of the new record. Neil Finn, Paul Hester and Nick Seymour began work on Crowded House's fourth album during Christmas 1992.

Having written and demoed material while on tour, they had several ideas that they could work with. They were tight as a band from their extensive touring, and this approach would serve them well as a unit for the recordings. They felt that this was the time to try something different in terms of their approach to recording an album.

Together Alone was mainly recorded at Neil Finn's friends Nigel and Jody Harrocks' house at Karekare Beach, a small coastal settlement in West Auckland, New Zealand. It was a house built on land owned by Sir Edmund Hillary, the first man to scale Everest. American actor Harvey Keitel stayed there when he was in Karekare to film Jane Campion's Oscar-winning *The Piano*. For Neil, recording the album in New Zealand was a chance to continue reconnecting with his homeland.

> I'd reconnected with New Zealand on the previous tour somehow and just thought, we can do anything we want now—why don't we just make a record in a house, somewhere out in the back blocks of New Zealand, the vibe will be good. I spent a month looking for a house. Went to Great Barrier Island with Jaz Coleman and got ferried across a swollen river in a flood by Jaz. We didn't find anywhere at the Great Barrier, but I looked all around Karekare. It was a solid idea, but for the life of me, now, I can't imagine why I was so possessed with that thought. We found a good house and we moved there. We carried the desk up to the house—all of us except Paul—and it was a really heavy desk, up this steep driveway. There was a lot of commitment involved.[1]

Seymour described the set-up at Karekare as 'like a co-operative campsite'. He said it was the first time he and the band had felt 'stateless… like we didn't belong anywhere'.[2] One of the considerations for the choice was to record the album as far away from the music industry as they could get.

As the journalist David Hepworth noted in the deluxe edition liner notes: 'Karekare was chosen because it was far enough from Auckland to ensure that nobody was going to come out, look over their shoulders and tell them they didn't hear a single.'[3]

The album sounds in places where it was recorded live with the band all in the same room. It was for the first week or so, then the band spread out around the various rooms of the house. Some even took to playing and recording outside when the weather allowed.

Additional recording took place in Melbourne, at both Periscope and Platinum Studios, but the bulk of it was recorded at Karekare.

Multi-instrumentalist Mark Hart had augmented the traditional line-up of Neil Finn, Nick Seymour and Paul Hester. He was listed as an additional musician on *Woodface* and had been around at the time of *Temple of Low Men*, but was now a full-time member of the band.

It wasn't just the formation of the band that changed; they opted for a different producer to record the album. Mitchell Froom had made a telling contribution to their previous albums, but for album number four, Neil felt that recording mainly in LA and Melbourne had become familiar and sterile for the band. He wanted to shake things up.

> Also, it struck me that the combination with Mitchell Froom, although I have nothing but good things to say about him, had become a little stale and conservative. I was sick of being called a well-crafted, well-mannered pop group.[4]

They had several producers who came forward offering their services, some names much sought after by other bands. Steve Lillywhite, notable for his work with U2 and many other bands, was one name that the band rejected. Another was John Leckie, whose CV included bands such as XTC, Pink Floyd and The Stone Roses. In the end, the band decided on the more leftfield choice of Martin 'Youth' Glover. The Killing Joke bassist has worked with several acts over the years, notably Paul McCartney on their The Fireman collaboration.

He was chosen on the strength of his joint-rolling abilities as well as his previous track record. He also brought some eccentric practices to the proceedings, which had the desired results in the overall outcome for the album.

As Paul Hester observed:

> He was a bit different in the studio, too. If we did something rocking, he'd stomp around chanting 'Pa-gan! Pa-gan!' When we got onto the harmony singing, he'd make a circle of rocks and insist we stood inside it. Then there was this friend of his who came visiting with his crystals. I sort of got to like him, and one day I said, you know, 'Nice crystal, mate', which seemed to encourage him 'cos he said, 'Oh, would you like to see me flying saucer then? It's in the boot of my car.' And it was. All sorts of people were coming around with strange potions.[5]

After a few missteps, Neil Finn could see that Youth's alternative methods did eventually payoff:

> For the first week, I was shitting myself. I'd met Youth once, and on the first day, I found the engineer, Greg Hunter, collapsed on the settee with his great long lank British hair falling to the floor. They'd stopped off in Bali on the way and got sick. Classic pom thing to do, hit the beach straight away and turn into

> a lobster. I thought, Fuck, this is mental. But then, after a while, I found we'd recorded fifteen songs in a fortnight, and I realised it was working.[6]

The original album was released on 11 October 1993. A deluxe edition was released in November 2016, which includes some strong material unlucky not to be included on the final version of the album.

It was an album that did well both commercially and critically for the band. It was kept from the number one slot in Britain only by Meat Loaf's *His Ubiquitous Loafness* and, gallingly, pegged at the same position in Australia by Michael Crawford's new album ('All the mums are buying it').[7]

Despite just missing out on the number one spot in the UK, *Together Alone* was the second album that cemented the band in the British record-buying public's conscience.

Neil Finn reflected on the way that the UK had embraced the band:

> It's very funny that our standard bearer now, internationally, should be Britain, because when we were being embraced by America, Britain didn't want to know. I'd given up on you all. I thought you were weird and unknowable and scene-obsessed and dismissive of colonials. But in the end people are won round. Besides, there's nothing tougher or wilder than a good tune.[8]

The atmosphere of Karekare permeates the record, and the quality of the final album more than justifies the reasoning behind recording in New Zealand. Songs like the title track, 'Together Alone', would not have existed if the album had been recorded elsewhere. It is a surprise that the band have not gone back there to record or a similar setting in New Zealand. It is probably hard to bottle magic like that twice. Besides, Crowded House are not a band to do the same thing twice.

A lot of emotions were brought to the fore during the making of that album. It was apparent to everyone involved that *Together Alone* was much more than just a new Crowded House album: it captured a unique experience. What Neil did not realise was that it would be fourteen more years before he and the band would make another record.[9]

Nick Seymour was again in charge of the direction of the look for the album. He explained his thinking for the cover and overall design:

> This background is a portrait of Piggy Banks, who was the former beach foraging wild Sow now corralled at the end of the driveway to the house we had commandeered to record the album's foundation tracks in the wilds of New Zealand's Karekare valley. She was quite tame and affectionate...The front cover is a high gloss duco-painted plaster carving depicting the spiritual quest of the prophets cruising and pondering all manner of aesthetics, faiths and sciences, all covered in our studio chatter and musical journey: Ironically, I created this carving in Tchad Blake's Los Angeles garage.[10]

The original idea for the cover could have been more controversial. There was talk of including a picture of Muhammad in the cover art. Depictions of the Prophet in Islam have been a contentious issue down the years. As can be seen with the issues when *Charlie Hebdo*, the French satirical magazine, published a cartoon depiction. Thanks to the intervention of their friend, the songwriter Richard Thompson, whose knowledge of the doctrines of Islam comes from observing a strand known as Sufism, the potential issues they could face should they go ahead with the planned design were pointed out to them.

Together Alone is the band's most accomplished album, something Neil Finn stated on his *Fangradio* special. It can be listened to from start to finish without the desire to skip a track. Sadly (at the time) it looked like it would be the last album recorded by Crowded House. Despite the success that came with the album, the pressures that came with touring a successful album impacted the band. Drummer Paul Hester quit the band midway through the world tour on an energy-sapping string of dates in the US.

David Hepworth remarked on his time on the road with Crowded House and the factors that led to Paul Hester quitting the tour:

> It was a few days after the death of Kurt Cobain, an event that had a profound impact on him. He still did his ringmaster act on stage—Paul was always the prime mover behind the zany stuff that provided a welcome counterpoint to their often quite spiritual music—but once he was on the bus, he was withdrawn and didn't want to be interviewed. A couple of days later, he just upped and left in the middle of the tour. He was homesick and unhappy and had a skin too thin to deal with life on the road.[11]

Drummers are often the butt of the joke, but when bands lose rheir drummers, they often lose their momentum. That is especially true of Crowded House. At the time, Paul Hester was an integral part of the band, often the instigator of the joke, not the butt of it. It would be hard to envisage Crowded House without his presence.

The tracks

'Kare Kare'

Written by Neil Finn, Nick Seymour, Mark Hart, and Paul Hester
Duration: 3:17

There is something ethereal about the opening of the first song that announces the fourth album by Crowded House.

The trademark harmonies are present. The rumbling bass of Nick Seymour, allied with Paul Hester's pounding drum, which in this context sounds like a thunderstorm is just a few valleys away. The chiming guitar line and the slide guitars throughout do not sound like a typical Crowded House track. The guitar sounds like it has captured the elemental nature of the place. There is a languid percussion that adds to the chilled-out feel of the song.

The setting is evoked beautifully, and its elements act as the foundation for the sound of the album. Even if you have never been to Karekare (which I have not), the lyrics and the music of this opener paint a vivid picture of the place.

Neil Finn said, reflecting on the process of making the album:

> We sat in there and we watched the weather come flying in every day with big bruising clouds. It's an amazing place, beautiful, but quite a heavy place, so the atmosphere permeates the record. I don't think *Together Alone* makes any more sense, ever, to anybody, than when it's played in Karekare.[12]

This was a collaborative effort from the band; all the band members get credit on this one. There was a lot of jamming on this record to try and fashion some ideas, and this was one of those tracks.

'In My Command'

Written by Neil Finn
Duration: 3:44

The song opens with another allusion to the tempestuous weather, or is it about the circumstances of the recording? It opens with stabbed piano chords and a slightly discordant guitar line. Again, this is another marker that the band are attempting something different with this album.

There is an impassioned vocal in the verses from Neil Finn, which leads us on to one of those trademark Crowded House choruses. Some shrieks can be heard in the background that give the song a live-in-the-room feel. Even with the rawer sound, the trademark harmonies are present on the chorus. The harmonies almost sound angelic and choral. Tim Finn is one of the voices that is added to the mix.

This acts as the perfect counterpoint to the jagged nature of the instrumentation. Everything is quite dominant in the mix, although this is not a problem. These contrasts work well in the song.

The song fades out, which further suggests that the bulk of this was recorded live. It is a shame that a longer take of this could not be found on the deluxe edition.

This song was allegedly recorded in the nude by the band. I am sure there is a metaphorical allusion that could be drawn here.

'Nails In My Feet'

Written by Neil Finn
Duration: 3:39
Released as a single in November 1993

Nick Seymour's bass acts as the lead instrument throughout the song quite effectively. Maybe this is the bass-playing producer Youth's influence over proceedings. Seymour has said that he came to the fore as a bass player during the making of this record. Although it was interesting to hear him say on the *Fangradio* broadcast of *Together Alone* that he was not that enamoured by the producer's methods.

The guitar solo is discordant offset against the strumming in the background; again, it works well. Vocally, this is another beautiful arrangement, which builds to an effective coda.

The title sounds like it has biblical connotations, but as with every great songwriter, the prosaic can often be made to sound quite profound. The nods towards the crucifixion of Jesus Christ were something less religious. Neil had dreamed of owning a tennis court, but it required a great deal of maintenance; that's where the special shoes came in; to aerate his lawn back in Melbourne.

There is a reference to a 'savage review'. I wonder if this is a reference to Robert Christgau's indifferent review of *Temple of Low Men* in *The Village Voice*. This is something that has been mentioned by the band throughout their career.

It was the second single to be released from the album.

'Black And White Boy'

Written by Neil Finn
Duration: 4:00

'Black and White Boy' is another guitar-heavy four-to-the-floor number, but it did not start that way. It evolved from a ballad to a glam stomper, to something the writer and journalist Stuart Maconie describes as 'visceral modernist rock'.[13]

The chugging rhythm throughout is interspersed with a delicate guitar hook. The bass is more rudimentary on this one, but it locks into the drumming. This adds to the driving nature of the song. It is another one that sounds like a live take; the outro sounds like it has been cut in the middle of the jam.

The 'black and white boy' in question is the Finn family dog, Lester (who will get a few more mentions later on). The title was inspired by Sam Hunt, the New Zealand poet. He is a friend of Neil Finn and was invited for dinner at his home with the dog present. After numerous glasses of wine and plenty of good cheer, the poet went from being civil, and lovingly calling the dog black and white boy – even making poems about him – to telling the dog where to go, with more colourful and not very poetic language.

The lyrics deal with the yin and yang nature of someone's personality, and the song has been interpreted in several ways. It is thought that it might be about Paul Hester, who experienced emotional highs and lows during the recording of the album.

'Fingers Of Love'

Written by Neil Finn
Duration: 4:27
Released as a single in May 1994

After the run of more muscular musical songs, the pace drops with a delicate and blissed-out track. The opening strumming pattern gives way to chiming guitars.

The sound of the song is evocative of the place where it was written. This time, though, that place is many miles away from New Zealand.

As Neil Finn explains:

> I remember quite strongly; we were in Jamaica on a holiday. Naturally enough, I was enjoying some really good quality Jamaican weed, sat out on the balcony in the place we were renting with my guitar and watched the sun go down with these extraordinary shafts of light coming through the clouds.[14]

It has been remarked that the song has an overt sexual connotation, but this has been refuted by Finn. He says that the fingers of love are about the God rays coming down while watching the sun come down.

There is a great spiralling guitar solo that breaks the reverie of the song for a moment. Nick Seymour's bass, not for the first time on the album, keeps it all together. The outro has a woozy quality to it. It is not often that Crowded House get noodly, but this jam-like song fits the mood quite well.

The deluxe edition of the album has a couple of demos and an alternative take that mark the evolution of the song. On the alternative take, you can hear the instructions to the band from producer Youth and direction from Finn shaping the song.

'Pineapple Head'

Written by Neil Finn
Duration: 3:27
Released as a single in September 1994

As the book will detail later, Neil Finn's sons have become an integral part of the band.

This is probably one of the first father-son collaborations, albeit an unwitting one for his eldest son, as Neil Finn noted in an interview with *Salon* in February 2014:

> 'Pineapple Head', I wrote on the piano in Melbourne at our house in Melbourne, and it curiously came from our son. Liam had a fever; he had quite a bad flu, and he was feverish and asleep and dreaming quite loudly, and he came up with a few of the lines in there in his sleep. I think it was 'the getaway car' and 'the detective is flat', and so rather than tending to him, I ran downstairs and wrote

> those lines down and wrote the verse of that song. I got a bit of stick from my wife about. Liam's still hitting me up for some publishing on that one.[15]

Again, the bass is driving the song in harmony with a strummed guitar line. The delicate guitars, maybe mandolins, are being used to good effect. The interlude has a very effective bass interlude. The harmonies are great as ever. It is a catchy song. It sounds like a flute in the background, which adds to the woozy nature of the song.

It would have slotted in neatly on the band's previous releases and still fits the mood of this album. It is a bright number that is in no way a throwaway.

'Locked Out'

Written by Neil Finn
Duration: 3:18
Released as a single in January 1994

The mellower moments in the middle of the album give way again to another up-tempo guitar-led song. There is an insistent riff throughout that acts as the hook.

The song rattles along and links in well with its video, which they filmed in Wales, where they ran like crazy through the village and the back streets for a whole day with a cast of characters. The four band members were attached to a harness to prop them up. Nick Seymour's broke, and he fell to the ground; thankfully, he was not injured.

He did not get much sympathy from those present, as he noted when talking about the experience:

> I could have hurt myself, and I remember somebody in the crew bursting into hysterical laughter when it happened. Extraordinarily unprofessional, but at the same time—it was funny!16

Neil Finn has said that 'Locked Out' was inspired by *Bliss*, a book by Australian author Peter Carey.

It was released as a single in January 1994. The song was also included on the soundtrack to the 1994 American film *Reality Bites*.

'Private Universe'

Written by Neil Finn
Duration: 5:39
Released as a single in August 1994 (Europe) and October 1994 (Australia)

Private Universe opens with ambient street sounds, as the out-of-control sounding guitars of 'Locked Out' fade away. It sounds like a taxi driver is taking a fare. There is what sounds like a brief snippet of a wailing harmonica. In comes the log drumming and slide guitar, which are the familiar tones. From the urban setting of the opening bars, we are transported back to Karekare.

The song is beautifully evocative and subtly done. There are some great stripped-back acoustic versions of this performed by the band down the years, that show, even without all the embellishments, that at its core, this is a perfect song.

The outro feels quite meditative, and it would not outstay its welcome if it carried on a bit longer than its five-minute-and-thirty-eight-second duration.

An original and more primitive take on 'Private Universe' can be found on the 2016 deluxe edition. It had a swing feel which did not work. It shows again the way that Finn finds the gold in the song eventually.

Elements of the song can be found in 'The Same Language as Me' (Live), which was recorded in 1991 in Switzerland. This song was still in development when the band jammed it on stage a handful of times on tour. A year later, the bridge was transplanted into 'Private Universe'.

Neil Finn has said that the lyrics were inspired by his childhood and partly by the place where he wrote the song:

> The first verse is connected to my childhood, being up this apple tree, I used to climb and spy on the neighbours. It's also connected to the house we had in Melbourne, so there's a mid-life thing too. But it's also about your whole life and how you create your private domain. I don't know that it has a clear narrative, but it has a deep sense of atmosphere. Songs are an alternative reality, or they should be.[17]

It is certainly a contender as one of the peaks of the album, and it still sounds as vibrant today. It was released as a single in Australia with a radio edit. This cuts out the last ninety seconds of the song and the log drummers.

The title of the song has also lent its name to the fan community set up by the band in 2025.

'Walking On the Spot'

Written by Neil Finn
Duration: 2:55

An early version of this appears on the deluxe edition of their eponymous debut album. That version is a bit more upbeat than the piano-led version that appears on *Together Alone*.

The original opens with the metronomic rhythm of an early drum machine. The reflective melody is all there, but compared to the final version, the vocal is taken at an undignified jaunty pace.

On this version, there is a melodica that works well in conjunction with the piano. That part was played by Nick Seymour, who also adds a bassline that blends into the background.

Brushes in the background add to the subtlety and tenderness of the arrangement. There is a tender vocal arrangement throughout. The piano arrangement is beautiful too, with some gentle flourishes.

Some songs find their way when they are sped up, the qualities of this one come to the fore at a slower tempo. It feels at home on *Together Alone*, and the patience in getting this one right, three albums later, has paid off.

'Distant Sun'

Written by Neil Finn
Duration: 5:13
Released as a single in September 1993

The lead single from the album. It gave a hint to fans and casual observers of the sound of the new album. It acts as a perfect bridge from the songs that came before and what to expect from the album, hinting at the album as a whole. The song is both tender and robust in one. The guitar employs a variant of the 'Kiwi strum' in the intro, before it builds to chorus and bridges that have invited many an audience to sing along down the years.

Neil Finn talks about the inspiration for some of the lyrics:

> 'Seven worlds collide'... A lot of the time, the first lines that I get just pop out, so I do not really remember what happened with that. It is a reference to the Pleiades, the Seven Sisters, which I must have been talking about with somebody. It is a likely place for extra-terrestrials to come from, supposedly, for people who follow those kinds of leads, and it is a significant cosmological part of the night sky. Apart from that, I do not know really. 'Tell me all the things you would change; I do not pretend to know what you want'—It is just wanting to get to know somebody, the unknowability of people, and the different influences that come from way, way out there in the universe that we do not even know about.[18]

The 'seven worlds collide' line lent its name to the project, led by Neil Finn, that brought together several great musicians to tour and write, perform and record together over two fantastic albums. (See the Solo Years chapter for more on those albums.)

'Catherine Wheels'

Written by Neil Finn, Neil Finn and Nick Seymour
Duration: 5:13

On an album of many fine contributions, this is Nick Seymour's crowning glory. He added his bass to good effect to an old Neil Finn and Tim Finn demo. A demo version can be found on the *Woodface* deluxe edition and the Finn Brothers' two-disc *Needle Mythology* re-release in 2022, as well as a B-side on the Finn Brothers' 'Suffer Never' single.

Seymour rightly gets a co-writing credit on this one; it is his bassline that elevates the song. It is another blissed-out arrangement. I could happily listen to an extended cut of this track. Guitars and mandolins seem to accompany the bass. The slide wah-wah guitar is played in the fade-out. It is another that sounds like it stemmed from a jam

According to Neil Finn, the subject of the lyrics is a fantasy about the breakup of a very twisted affair.

'Skin Feeling'

Written by Paul Hester
Duration: 3:57

Musically, this is not a million miles away from U2's 'The Fly', which came out in the same period. The chugging Bo Diddly rhythm has been appropriated by many a band down the years, so much so that U2 lawyers did not get in touch to demand a royalty.

It is a Paul Hester number. It acts as a counterpoint to the chilled-out and rockier numbers throughout the album. The guitar solo sounds like it is about to fall apart at any moment, but it adds to the feel of the song.

Mark Hart is credited with the distorted commentary, 'I like to roll in the sand like a horse! I like to fly high like an eagle!', which appears at the end of the track.

'Together Alone'

Written by Neil Finn, Bub Wehi, and Mark Hart
Duration: 3:56

This is the perfect ending to an album that almost feels like the band's most complete effort. The distinctive sounds of New Zealand come to the fore again.

A lot is going on in the arrangement, but at no point does this overwhelm the song. A lot was going on with the recording, too.

Paul Hester conducted the log drummers. Neil looked after the choir. Mark led the brass with their part of the arrangement. The emotional part of the day for Neil Finn was when the drummers' families got involved. The Te Waka Huia Cultural Group Choir comprised sixty singers, but 300 people turned up on the day.

The recording captured a great deal of the ambient nature sounds of the valley. The crickets can be heard chirping along with the song.

Neil Finn has recounted what seems to have been a memorable occasion on his website:

> It was a memorable day when we did 'Together Alone'. It was an idea that came about during the recording of the album that we should try and write

> something to draw in what we saw as a few strands of New Zealand music. A Māori singing group was a pretty central part of the New Zealand experience. I was also very fond of brass bands when I grew up because they used to play on the back of trucks at Christmas time and come around. It was a sound I loved. The log drummers were something I'd become aware of only really in that period, although It is as old as the hills. We thought we'd unite them all and wrote a song based around that idea. Got together with Bub Wehi from Te Waka Huia, the Māori group in West Auckland. I gave him an idea of what the song should be about, and he wrote some lyrics. So it was well conceived, and I think it was a beautiful ending to the record.[19]

On the version that appears on the deluxe edition, there are an extra eighteen seconds of fade-out at the end of the track, compared to one on the original album. This may have been included by mistake. This happy accident captures one of the musicians having just recorded the song, and after the applause of the choir has died down, on what sounds like the perfect take, can be heard asking, 'But did you press the record button?'

Thankfully, someone had, and it had captured one of the band's greatest moments.

2016 Deluxe Edition bonus disc (Universal/Capitol)

The 2016 Deluxe Edition, again in keeping with previous releases, comes with an extra disc of songs that did not make the main album or are earlier versions of songs that made the final album.

Tracklist

'Blue Smoke' (home demo), 'Fingers Of Love' (writing demo), 'Private Universe' (home demo), 'The Same Language As Me' (live), 'Tail Of A Comet' (live), 'Distant Sun' (writing demo), 'I Am In Love' (band demo), 'Fingers Of Love' (band demo), 'Fingers Of Love' (alternative studio take), 'Black And White Boy'(early rough mix), 'Locked Out' (Zen mix), 'Newcastle Jam' (studio version), 'Convent Girls' (studio version), 'Zen Roxy'.

5

Recurring Dream: The Very Best of Crowded House (1996)

Original album released in June 1996

Personnel:	Nick Seymour: bass and vocals Neil Finn: guitars and vocals Mark Hart: guitars, keyboard and vocals All songs written by Neil Finn except: 1, 13, 14, by Neil Finn and Tim Finn, and 16, by Neil Finn and Mitchell Froom Tracks 2, 5, 6, 8, 12, 16, 17 and 18 produced by Mitchell Froom Tracks 3, 13 and 14 produced by Neil Finn and Mitchell Froom, recorded by Tchad Blake Track 1 was produced by Neil Finn and Mitchell Froom Tracks 4, 7, 9 and 15 produced by Youth, engineered by Greg Hunter, mixed by Bob Clearmountain for Fast Forward Productions Ltd. Tracks 10, 11 and 12 produced by Mitchell Froom, Tchad Blake and Neil Finn All tracks performed by Crowded House (Neil Finn, Nick Seymour and Mark Hart) with Paul Hester and (on tracks 1, 13 and 14) Tim Finn. 'Not The Girl You Think You Are', 'Instinct', and 'Everything Is Good For You' recorded at York St Studios, Auckland, New Zealand
Duration:	70:10
Produced by:	Mitchell Froom, Tchad Blake and Neil Finn
Chart positions:	Australia: 1; New Zealand: 1; UK: 1

Instead of shaping the way for a new direction, *Together Alone* and the subsequent tour saw the end of Crowded House. Paul Hester's leaving the band had fundamentally changed things for the band. There was a tentative plan in place to release a new album, with the working title 'Help is Coming'. The initial sessions included Hester's replacement, Peter Jones, but that project was shelved as Neil Finn's mind turned to solo projects. He was also working on the long-awaited first Finn Brothers album at the time, so his focus was elsewhere. Mark Hart and Nick Seymour were surprised; they felt that the band had one more album in them.

After four albums and a major line-up change, it felt right for an album to be released that would sum up the first phase of the band. The announcement was supposed to come at a fan club-only gig in London at the Hanover Grand on 3 June 1996, but Neil Finn could not find a way of making the announcement.

It was at a press conference in the following days that they announced the band's intention to split and the release of Recurring Dream: The Very Best of Crowded House. The June concerts in Europe and Canada would be their final shows.[1]

The title *Recurring Dream* comes from a song long known to fans. It is one that the band have played live on many occasions down the years, even as far back as when they were called The Mullanes. It has been used as a B-side; it even featured on the soundtrack of the 1988 movie *Tequila Sunrise*. The track was not an extra song on this collection; it would eventually find a home on an album in the *Afterglow* extras collection.

As with most compilations, there is always an addition of something to keep the diehard fans happy. In this case, three new tracks were included on the album. Importantly, the whole gang was there for one last mission. Paul Hester returned on drums, so too did their trusted producers from the first three albums.

These new tracks were recorded at York St Studios, Auckland, New Zealand, with Mitchell Froom and Tchad Blake on production duties, along with Neil Finn.

Reflecting on the 1996 sessions for the *Recurring Dream* compilation, he said, 'There was a working environment that had a lovely feel to it. You know, a feeling of putting on an old coat and finding a tenner in the pocket. It was nice to get the old team back for that one.'[2]

The front cover featured another painting by Nick Seymour, in what looks like something of a self-portrait. Along with a red car, the cover also features an electric fan, an item which appeared on the sleeve of their eponymous debut album.

Tracklist

'Weather With You', 'World Where You Live', 'Fall at Your Feet', 'Locked Out', 'Don't Dream It's Over', 'Into Temptation', 'Pineapple Head', 'When You Come',

'Private Universe', 'Not The Girl You Think You Are', 'Instinct', 'I Feel Possessed', 'Four Seasons In One Day', 'It's Only Natural', 'Distant Sun', 'Something So Strong', 'Mean To Me', 'Better Be Home Soon', and 'Everything Is Good For You'.

In addition to these tracks, the three new songs were as follows:

'Not The Girl You Think You Are'

Written by Neil Finn
Duration: 4:09
Released as a single in November 1996

It has a melancholic feel to it that often comes from songs by bands that have announced their intention to split up. Lyrically, the song reads like it is talking about a deception, for instance, 'They're not his shoes under your bed', which comes from a phrase a family member of Neil Finn would say. The reviews had noted the song's Beatlesque quality, something that Finn had strived for when writing this one.

There is something classic about this song. The style in which it was written and the way that it was recorded all feel that this is from another age. The haunting piano loop is from Neil's trusty old-school Optigan keyboard – it has helped with a few other songs down the years.

> I found this neat little piano loop on the Optigan, which features in "Not The Girl You Think You Are", and the finished song is arranged as my little demo at home was [this can be heard on the bonus disc of the Afterglow album]. There are about thirty Optigan discs available with all sorts of exotic sounds, but very low fidelity, and I've plundered the catalogue now. I've got a lot of songs out of it, so it was a hundred bucks well spent.[3]

This was released as a standalone single in 1996, back in the days of the multiple format releases. The two-part single was backed by several live tracks recorded on the Phill Jupitus show, BBC GLR, 21 June 1996. These were the last performances in the UK of the first phase of the band. These included 'Instinct' (live), 'Distant Sun' (live), 'Fall at Your Feet' (live), 'Private Universe' (live), 'Fingers of Love' (live) and 'Better Be Home Soon' (live).

'Instinct'

Written by Neil Finn
Duration: 3:08
Released as a single in June 1996

This is driven by a pounding Nick Seymour bassline, which also acts as the lead hook. This stems from a demo that Neil Finn put together, with this element in the foreground. The drums lock in and help to give the song its driving beat. Although understated, the guitars also lock in to help the song along. The extended outro sounds like this might have been a live take of the song, with all the band coming to the fore with their contributions. There sounds like a glockenspiel in the mix, too. It is quite a laid-back number.

The line 'I lit the match and saw another monster turn to ash' could well be reflective of feelings towards Crowded House's impending split.

It is another song that was moulded from a rough demo that to other ears may have felt like it was going nowhere. Neil Finn knew there was something in the initial idea that he put down:

> I wrote it in the studio one night. That was another where I sang a nonsense version and used made-up sounds. But then I listen through and garner a few lines out of the gabble, which become the basis of the song. Sometimes it's difficult because you get so attracted to the sound of the words, you leave them like that because you can't find a way to make them make sense. I made sense of it as best I could.[4]

This is the most commercial of the three new songs recorded for this compilation. It just missed the top ten in the UK by two places. This was released as a standalone single in 1996; again, it is backed by several tracks. The two-part single was backed by several live tracks and interesting curios, including, 'Recurring Dream', the remix from the *Tequila Sunrise* soundtrack. Live takes of 'Weather with You', 'Chocolate Cake', which features elements of The Beatles' 'Rocky Raccoon', 'World Where You Live', 'In the Lowlands' and 'Into Temptation'. As well as an alternative mix of 'Instinct'.

'Everything Is Good for You'

Written by Neil Finn
Duration: 3:52
Released as a single in 1996.

Poignantly, Paul Hester can be heard counting this one in. It is quite an innocuous-sounding song at first, but the hooky guitar gets under the skin with repeated spins. There is a scuzzy spiralling riff at the outro that highlights a band at the top of their game.

Nick Seymour's bass can be heard pushing the song along, not for the first time on a Crowded House number. Sadly, at this point, it would seem that we would not hear this again. It is one of those inconspicuous songs that the band do well. To me, it is the pick of the three new tunes on the compilation. Lyrically, the song is about not letting regrets ruin your life.

The last song on the compilation and the first single to be released to promote *Recurring Dream,* it came with live versions of 'History Never Repeats' (credited as Pearl Jam with the Finn Brothers) and 'Chocolate Cake'. A great live version of this track can be found on the *Farewell to the World* album.

Recurring Dream: Special Edition Live Album

This was a limited-edition bonus disc released in June 1996. It was compiled by Nigel Griggs. Neil Finn invited him to pull together a live compilation from multiple sources. It was a chance to feature some lesser-known cuts, such as 'Newcastle Jam', a *Together Alone*-era song, that had never been heard before in this form.

Tracklist

'There Goes God', 'Newcastle Jam', 'Love You 'Til the Day I Die', 'Hole In The River', 'Private Universe', 'Pineapple Head', 'How Will You Go', 'Left Hand', 'Whispers And Moans', 'Kill Eye', 'Fingers Of Love', 'Don't Dream It's Over', 'When You Come', 'Sister Madly', 'In My Command'

6

Afterglow (1999)

Original album release:	December 1999
Deluxe Edition release:	November 2016
Produced by:	Mitchell Froom, Tchad Blake, Neil Finn, Crowded House, and Youth
Duration:	Original 1999 album 47:10; (2016) Deluxe Edition second disc: 48:00
Chart positions:	Australia: 36; New Zealand: 30

As you would expect with a songwriter with the prodigious talents of Neil Finn, there would be a few off-cuts to be found on hard drives and shelves somewhere.

In the days of two-part CD releases and when single releases were a physical entity, there was a need to come up with more tracks to bulk out those editions. Crowded House (and their label) often opted for live tracks to fill the extra tracks, but there was always an abundance of other interesting curios that never made the final releases.

As a band, they were known to road test unreleased tracks during gigs. Some of these have never been included on any previous album. This collection was a good opportunity to assemble these and give them the spotlight they deserve.

Afterglow came out in 1999 in the days before streaming took off, as a way to collate those other tracks. Most fans would prefer to have these on a physical edition anyway. There is an abundance of material that makes for a coherent album in its own right, despite being recorded at many points in the band's career.

This album was partly released because fans of the band questioned Neil Finn about obscure tunes and B-sides and how they could get hold of them. In some cases, fans had cited some of these curios as being among their favourite

Crowded House tracks. It was a chance for Finn to reflect on why some of these songs had been omitted from albums.

After playing a live take of 'Anyone Can Tell' (formerly a B-side and available now on *Afterglow*) on episode 18 of his *Fangradio* show in May 2020, he talked in general about some of the songs that initially missed out on albums: 'Some of the best things that we have done have ended up on the bonus discs of the repackaged Crowded House albums.'[1]

Neil Finn's reflective commentaries on his website give a great insight into why some did not get included at the time. He talks about curious omissions that, in hindsight, could have seen the light of day long before this release.

An expanded edition released in 2016 included more missing tracks, as well as demos and embryonic songs that appear on Finn's solo albums.

The artwork, as ever, was Nick Seymour's area; he talked about the inspirations at the time of the release of the deluxe edition:

> It was a combination from my journal of an image I had of the brownstone tenement buildings in Brooklyn, New York, that I'd drawn when touring and then one of the portraits I'd done of a studio control room. The hands were an image I did in the studio again, an image of falling down some stairs. It's a combination of elements. It wasn't with anything particularly in mind. There's a big joint being passed in the hands. There are a couple of other black-and-white drawings that went with that album, but again, it was just ideas thrown together with a deadline in mind for release.[2]

The tracks

'I Am in Love'

Written by Neil Finn
Duration: 4:38

This is certainly a song that should be filed under the 'ones that got away' category. This had the potential to be included on an earlier album. It had been previously released as an extra track on the 'Nails in My Feet' and 'Private Universe' singles, but it earns its place on this best-of-the-rest collection. It is a song that the band have played live throughout their career.

This was recorded during the *Together Alone* sessions at Karekare Beach with Youth producing. As with many of the songs from that period, it came together as a live take. As Neil explains:

> Mark, Paul, Nick and Neil Finn all sat 'round, Mark and I sitting outside the glass doors with our guitars, Paul in the lounge room with the drums, and Nick stuck up in the bedroom there right next to his bass amp, the way he liked it,' noted how the song came about.[3]

It was one of the first songs that was recorded and one that, in the eyes of Finn, should have made the album: 'Don't really know why it didn't, except we had a lot of songs, nineteen in all. Perhaps I was a little sheepish about the title being so direct, but really, no particular reason it didn't make *Together Alone*.'[4]

Sonically, it shares a lot of the atmosphere and style of *Together Alone*; it would have fitted in well with that album. There is a jangly guitar as the hook throughout. There is another of those catchy choruses that sneaks up on you. As per the producer Youth's instructions, Nick Seymour's bass does not do too much walking about and sticks to one string to deliver something that propels the song along. You can understand the dilemma of the band. This is a good track, but what could be omitted to find a home for it?

A home recording of the initial demo also appears on the deluxe edition. This is rudimentary, as you would expect with a demo, but the potential of the song is definitely there.

'Sacred Cow'

Written by Neil Finn
Duration: 3:37

A song that did not make it onto *Woodface*. Material was abundant at the time, what with the simultaneous Crowded House and Finn Brothers sessions going on.

The melody of the verse and some of the lyrics came from 'You Got Me Going', a home demo of which was recorded in 1989 on an eight-track. A version of this can be heard on the deluxe box set of *Woodface*; it is a version that Neil Finn has a fondness for. This may explain his desire to rework it.

The song that appears on this album comes from a couple of other tracks, and it was again Mitchell Froom's intervention that realised the potential of a couple of ideas and made them into something better.

The chorus belonged to the unreleased song 'Cigarette Girl'. The intro featured appeared on tape as 'Sax Boogie', an instrumental four-track demo, featuring a keyboard saxophone.

Musically, it is a song that Neil Finn has grown to love, but at the time, he was not sure of the lyrical content of the song, which may have counted against it being released before now: 'I had no idea what the hell the song meant. Sacred cows, jealous rage, and religious objects. You know, what does it all mean?'[5]

The melody is quite catchy in itself. There is a nice guitar riff that runs throughout the song that gives it its hook. The breakdown for the middle eight is a jazzy interlude, with the 'Sax Boogie' demo incorporated in this section.

'You Can Touch'

Written by Neil Finn
Duration: 3:47

It has the sound that was synonymous with the *Together Alone* sessions. There was an added grit to the trademark polished sounds of Crowded House at this point in their existence, something the band utilised to good effect on their fourth album.

The song stemmed from a particularly fractious session that ran late into the night. Paul Hester took exception to Neil Finn's instruction as to how the drum beat of the song should go. He stormed out of the studio and left Finn to do it himself. As Neil Finn explains:

> I was a bit stubborn and decided that I could do the drums myself, and proceeded to record five tracks of mono drums, which I thought sounded pretty good. The opening fill to this day sounds very exciting to my ears, but unfortunately, Bob Clearmountain, who mixed the album, didn't really agree. In fact, I remember him coming in to see me halfway through the mix of this one and saying, 'Neil, I really like your voice, I really like your guitar playing and your songs, but I can't mix your drums.[6]

Paul Hester's contributions did make it onto the record; his overdubbed drums can be heard in the outro of the song, starting just after the three-minute mark.

The song feels quite laid-back throughout the verses, and the break adds to the effect. The song takes off after about a minute as the drums kick in. The guitar riff comes in and out of the mix to good effect.

This is another one that seems unfairly to have been left off the final cut of the album. It was previously featured on the 'Nails in My Feet' single, as well as on a Spanish promotional CD.

'Help Is Coming'

Written by Neil Finn, Nick Seymour, and Peter Jones
Duration: 4:49

This is one of the last songs the band recorded before they broke up. It was recorded at York Street Studios in Auckland with Peter Jones, the band's then drummer. He gets a co-write on this one. Other songs were written and recorded in this period for what could have been the band's fifth album. They were included on the *Recurring Dream* compilation album as extra tracks. The title was even suggested as a working title for a potential new album.

Again, the song was destined to have never been heard, but has had an interesting second and third life since then: initially, as part of this collection, and then when released as a limited-edition charity 7-inch single in 2015.

The broadcasters/writers Caitlin Moran and Pete Paphides were angered by images of three-year-old Alan Kurdi and his brother Galip caught up in the Syrian refugee crisis of 2015.

Peter Paphides had an idea how they could help:

> I started imagining my family in a similar situation, and almost without me realising it, a song I hadn't heard for several years started playing in my head. "Help Is Coming" was recorded by Crowded House over 20 years ago, but it evokes with uncanny empathy the howling uncertainty faced by thousands of families arriving in Europe for the first time. The following day, I contacted friends at The Vinyl Factory—a label that owns the old EMI pressing plant in Hayes—with a view to manufacturing a seven-inch single with all the proceeds going to Save the Children. They responded immediately, offering to waive all their manufacturing costs.[7]

As well as being for a good cause, it is an object lesson of how songs find their way eventually, as Neil Finn has noted:

> I am continually amazed and grateful for the mysterious pathways that songs can travel. You never know where they are going to turn up and when they will reveal their true nature. First recorded in 1995, quietly released in 1999, 'Help Is Coming' has had a long journey to find a good home. It was always a song about refugees, even if at the time I was thinking about the immigrants setting off on ships from Europe to America, looking for a better life for their families in America. The words of the poem inscribed on the Statue of Liberty are an extraordinary statement of intent for the development of a great nation: 'Give me your tired, your poor, your huddled masses yearning to breathe free.'[8]

It is a dreamy, shimmering, delicate number. The slide guitars act as the hook throughout. There is a trademark Nick Seymour bassline walking through this song. It is buried in the mix, but it is distinctive. It highlights the evolution of the band's sound during the *Together Alone* sessions.

'I Love You Dawn'

Written by Neil Finn
Duration: 2:34

It is a song that might have been in the running for *Woodface*, but given the inclusion of the songs originally intended for a Finn brothers album, it was relegated to languish in the best-of-the-rest category.

It was one of the first songs that the band had recorded in the period after *Temple of Low Men*. It is a song that Neil Finn has always liked and not just because of the lyrical matter: 'It's kind of special because it's a song I wrote for my wife, Sharon Dawn, and quite a direct song for me.'[9]

It is a charming number; maybe its omission may have something to do with the verse sounding rhythmically like a slowed-down version of 'Weather With You'.

It was released as a Spanish promo CD single in 1999 as part of the launch of this album.

'Dr Livingstone'

Written by Neil Finn
Duration: 3:57

The song was inspired by a trip Neil Finn took to Mozambique, visiting refugee camps. He was there at the invitation of an aid agency when he did some PR for them.

He has noted the lyrical inspirations:

> It was a very obviously affecting experience being in Africa, especially in a ravaged part of Africa, Mozambique at the time, which was in the middle of a civil war. I wrote this song as a result. It's a series of images of what I'd seen. I was always really fond of the song and the rhythm track in particular. In the end, I think it didn't make the record because I wasn't sure I should be singing songs about those kind of issues. I've always tended to keep messages or social commentary out of my songs and prefer the more personal statement. But it's well deserving of a place on *Afterglow*.[10]

Musically, it sounds like it would have worked as well as part of the *Woodface* album. It has a verse that ticks along nicely until the chorus builds with the impassioned Finn vocal. There is a great deal of singing to fit in, another reason why it appears on this album.

The subject of the song, Dr David Livingstone, was a missionary and explorer famous for his expeditions. On one such journey, he went missing and was tracked down by the Welsh-American journalist Henry Morton Stanley, who greeted Livingstone on the shore of Lake Tanganyika with his famous line, 'Dr Livingstone, I presume?' He'd gone off to search for the source of the Nile, but had gone missing, presumed dead, for six years.

The song was previously available on the 'It's Only Natural' and 'Four Seasons in One Day' singles.

'My Telly's Gone Bung'

Written by Paul Hester
Duration: 3:14

Another Paul Hester song that covers one of his favourite pastimes, watching TV.

The cultural references include Kylie and Jason, who were just breaking through at the time with the TV show *Neighbours* in Australia. That programme was successfully syndicated around the world. Both have gone on to have sustained careers. Kylie is more internationally famous with her continued pop career.

'I can't remember why this did not make it either. Probably just the competition got too hot for *Woodface*,' Neil Finn has said about the song.[11]

It is a great bit of whimsy from the pen of Paul Hester. There is a country vibe to it. There may even be a bit of cowbell in the mix. There is a great bit of Hammond organ throughout the song. The piano break works well.

Possibly lost out in a toss-up between this and 'Italian Plastic' in the running order for *Woodface*. A tough choice.

'Private Universe'

Written by Neil Finn
Duration: 4:09

A different take from the version released on *Together Alone*. It sounds like it is a finger-picked number with Finn delivering a tender version of the song stripped of the Polynesian backing track. There is a beautifully haunting harmony throughout the song. A lovely alternative take, Neil Finn has performed this version live many times, especially on his *Fangradio* shows.

'Lester'

Written by Neil Finn
Duration: 2:19

A song about not taking the family pet for granted.

The Finn family Dalmatian was also the inspiration for the song 'Black and White Boy', as detailed in the *Together Alone* chapter. He was an ever-present with the family for so long that he even made cameo appearances in the band's 'Weather with You' and 'Everything Is Good for You' videos. He can even be seen running around in one of the documentary extras on the *Farewell to the World* DVD.

This is quite a sparse arrangement, still in its original demo form. That fits the lyrical tone of the song. It is an affectionate ode to their dog that was written about an accident that nearly killed him outside their family home.

'Lester is a home demo I recorded in 1988 shortly after getting our dog, Lester, a Dalmatian, who came to grief on the road outside our house in Melbourne with a Jeep,' Neil Finn has said about the song.[12]

It is a song that has even had several outings at live gigs down the years. It is often requested by fans when Neil Finn does his online gigs. It is a song that he likes, but it was felt that it might be a bit too sentimental to make the running for *Woodface*.

The band now release their records on the Lester Records imprint, a further tribute to Neil's beloved dog.

'Anyone Can Tell'

Written by Neil Finn
Duration: 3:36

Another song that was in the running for the *Woodface* album did not make the final selection. It is another song that Mitchell Froom helped shape from a couple of other ideas.

The opening riff has echoes of 'Recurring Dream', the song that follows on this compilation. Neil Finn was not quite sure of the lyrics at the time, but he mellowed to it down the years: 'I probably never quite came to terms with the lyrical match-up, but I can listen to it now quite happily in all its ambiguity.[13]

It was another song that Neil pulled out of the bag for one of his *Fangradio* lockdown shows.

'Recurring Dream'

Written by Neil Finn, Paul Hester, Nick Seymour and Craig Hooper
Duration: 3:25

This is the ultimate one that got away. 'Recurring Dream' is a song that still to this day appears in the band's live set. It is a song that predates Crowded House and stems from the days of The Mullanes. The song owes a lot to their former guitarist, who left to rejoin his old band before the recording of the eponymous debut album.

Neil Finn said about the song:

> We have to give Craig Hooper a lot of credit for 'Recurring Dream' because the two-guitar part that we had was very much him and me at rehearsals in a jammy kind of mode. We were rehearsing at Factory Sound in South Melbourne. We wrote it there and might have recorded a demo of it there as well, and then we did another demo some other time.[14]

The opening riff is perfect and elements of this return throughout the song. The twin guitar jangle is catchy. Some bands would kill to write a song as good and as hooky as this. At last, it has been given the outing it deserves. It should, in all honesty, have appeared earlier and not just as a B-side.

A song called 'Hoedown', which is an instrumental version of this song, remains unreleased. That was recorded back in 1985/86. Elements of it can be heard in the bass solo that falls in the middle of the final version of 'Recurring Dream', a part of the song often extended when played live, giving Seymour the spotlight.

'Recurring Dream' has appeared in numerous places over the years, notably on the soundtracks to the 1988 films *Tequila Sunrise* and *Rikky & Pete*. It did not appear on the 1996 *Recurring Dream* compilation album, but it did appear on the deluxe double-disc version of *The Very, Very Best of Crowded House*, a compilation released by their former label EMI/Capitol at the end of the band's contract in 2010.

It can also be found on *Crowded House—Box Set (Deluxe Edition)*, as well as the 'Instinct' and 'Now We're Getting Somewhere' singles.

'Left Hand'

Written by Neil Finn
Duration: 2:57

This is a song that is no stranger to fans of Crowded House. It would also be a familiar tune to those lucky fans who managed to see The Mullanes back in the day. An earlier version of Left Hand was performed in gigs by The Mullanes as far back as 1985. Crowded House have released several live cuts of the song down the years.

This version was recorded at Tim Finn's Periscope Studios and captures the essence of the song well. It is unpolished in its form here. The bass line is the hook, and it is another excellent workout from Nick Seymour. The bass locks in well with the wah-wah guitar employed throughout.

The verse was once married to the chorus of 'Fall at Your Feet', before Mitchell Froom had his way. Also, Paul Hester's 'Creek Song' (aka 'Song for Mulga') had elements of 'Left Hand' in its early incarnations.

Neil Finn is unsure what the song is about even to this day: 'There are some songs that fall into the I-don't-know-what-they're-about-category, and that's definitely one of them.'[15]

'Time Immemorial'

Written by Neil Finn
Duration: 4:07

It is another of the early demos that were written for *Woodface*. This is one that Finn liked, but Mitchell Froom thought '...it sounded a bit too folky'.[16] That is why the song was not released before now.

There are some interesting diversions musically that lift this song beyond a simple folk song. The Hammond keyboard and the piano vamping at the end elevate the song. There sounds like a harmonium on there, to go along with the delicately strummed guitar. The verse leads to a trademark Crowded House hooky chorus. Neil Finn has played the song live on his *Fangradio* broadcasts, and the essence of the tune lends itself to being stripped back and played in this way.

Could it have made *Woodface*? Neil Finn has talked about that album being two songs too many. With that in mind, it is hard to see what you'd drop in favour of it, but it certainly deserves to be released as part of this package.

2016 Deluxe Edition bonus disc (Capitol/Universal)

The original album *Afterglow* was given the deluxe treatment in 2016, with extra demos and other unreleased songs. There are more interesting curios on the deluxe edition: a few versions of the songs that appeared on the original album, ones that appeared on the *Recurring Dream* compilation, some that have never been released before.

'I Am In Love' (home demo)

Written by Neil Finn
Duration: 2:08

The original appears on disc one of the album. A stripped-back version recorded with a drum machine and guitar track.

'Instinct' (home demo)

Written by Neil Finn
Duration: 2:04

The original version of the song was released as a single; it was also one of three extra tracks that appeared on the *Recurring Dream* compilation album. 'Instinct' is a song that was recorded during the session for extra tracks for the *Recurring Dream* compilation album. It is a more laid-back take on the song. The recognisable melody is still there.

'Spirit Of The Stairs' (home demo)

Written by Neil Finn
Duration: 3:41

Another one that had potential and did not make the cut for the original album. 'Spirit of the Stairs' is a literal translation of the French idiom *l'esprit de l'escalier*: 'It's the thoughts you have as you leave a difficult situation and think of all the things that you should have said, and it's a very nice idea for a song.'[17]

The song was written in 1995, and it makes you wonder if the lyrics are an oblique reference to thoughts Neil Finn was having about the future of the band. Musically, it sounds in keeping with the style that shaped *Together Alone*. There is a looseness to the song, big on atmospherics. The guitar riff is off-kilter in a good way. It sounds like some of the soundtrack music that Finn has written throughout his career.

'I'm So Scared of Losing I Can't Compete' (home demo)

Written by Neil Finn
Duration: 2:11

Another one written in 1995, it could have been a contender for an album to follow up *Together Alone* or as extra tracks for the compilation that followed. It is one that Neil Finn is surprised they did not do more with:

> 'I like that chorus. I'm amazed I never pulled that out and did anything with it. 'I'm so scared of losing, I can't compete.' That's a good line, I think.[18]

There is a great nagging guitar line throughout. The chorus is great too. The song was very much in its infancy here, but it is clear to see that this had the potential to be something more than being confined to this extras collection.

'Everything Is Good for You' (home demo)

Written by Neil Finn
Duration: 3:15

The original was released as a single; it was also one of three extra tracks that appeared on the *Recurring Dream* compilation album. Here it is in its embryonic form.

'Not The Girl You Think You Are' (home demo)

Written by Neil Finn
Duration: 3:01

The original was released as a single; it was also one of three extra tracks that appeared on the *Recurring Dream* compilation album. It is another sparse demo arrangement, yet it sounds fully formed, not far off from the version that was released.

'Anthem'

Written by Neil Finn
Duration: 3:31

This is the song that appeared on the B-side of the 'Help Is Coming' 7-inch single released in September 2015. Although it was not written to back the charity single, lyrically it effectively complements it.

It is one of the songs from the 1995 sessions that the band recorded with Peter Jones on drums. There was a vocal overdub in 2015 for the B-side release. This is one that had great potential. A new Crowded House album at that time would have had some great songs, as the demos and missing tracks across *Afterglow* highlight.

There is a slow build in the verse to a distinct chorus. There is a laid-back feel to the rhythmical elements of the verse. The harmonies add to the hook of the song. It has a classic Crowded House sound.

'I Don't Know You' (studio demo)

Written by Mark Hart
Duration: 3:40

Paul Hester and Tim Finn have typically taken the lead on Crowded House songs; this was the first time that Mark Hart got the chance to sing lead vocals. This is a solo number and was part of the 1995 recording sessions in Auckland.

On first listen, it sounds like a Crowded House number. There is a lithe percussion throughout. Nick Seymour plays one of his great expressive basslines that underpins the song. The harmonies act as a great hook. The vocals are great throughout.

It was later re-recorded by Mark and released on his debut solo album, *Nada Sonata*, in 2001.

'Taste Of Something Divine' (studio demo)

Written by Neil Finn, Nick Seymour, Mark Hart, Peter Jones and Paddy Free
Duration: 4:14

A song that sounds like a precursor to what has followed with Neil Finn's solo career. It would also have been an interesting direction for Crowded House to have taken with their new album if this had been released at the time. For a band that, in its first incarnation, was associated with a more elemental style of recording, an electronic edge would have been a great direction for them to take.

It is another one from the 1995 sessions; it features the four-piece band at the time, augmented by New Zealand electronic musician Paddy Free.

Neil Finn has highlighted how the band's capacity to jam was involved in the process of putting this one together:

> There was a lot of electronic stuff happening at the time. As a traditional four-piece band, we were interested in that process. We jammed it a lot and then went through and sampled bits from the jam that we liked. We laid out all these samples on a keyboard and then played a structure down, and I made some loose vocals. There was an album after that, Try Whistling This, that I made solo, where Paddy got involved as well.[19]

Neil Finn's vocals and lyrics have a blissed-out quality. Nick Seymour's bass acts almost like the lead instrument here. The guitar line comes and goes throughout the song. The electronic bed is the hook of the song.

'Spirit Of The Stairs' (studio demo)

Written by Neil Finn
Duration: 4:57

This is a longer, more polished take of the song that has already appeared on the collection. The studio demo, again, highlights the band's capacity to jam. The extended break at the end shows that this would have been a great one to have heard the band perform live.

'Loose Tongue' (rough mix)

Written by Neil Finn
Duration: 3:51

This was recorded in the same spirit as 'Taste of Something Divine'. This was recorded by the reunited original three members of the band along with producers Mitchell Froom and Tchad Blake.

Neil Finn said that at some point, it was in the running to make the compilation album:

> We did a version of that at the same session as 'Not The Girl You Think You Are' and 'Instinct'. I think at the time, I didn't think we'd quite got the definitive version, so it got left aside. We also only needed two or three songs, so we probably ran out of room.[20]

There is a looseness and a swagger to this one. The rough cut of the song shows the band in good form in the studio. The guitar riff acts as the hook, while the percussive elements drive the song along. An interesting hint of what was to come from Neil Finn. A version of this would eventually find a home on Neil Finn's debut album *Try Whistling This*, which was released in 1998, with a Jim Moginie co-write credit.

'Instinct'

Written by Neil Finn
Duration: 3:06

'Everything Is Good for You'

Written by Neil Finn
Duration: 3:52

'Not The Girl You Think You Are'

Written by Neil Finn
Duration: 4:10

'Instinct', 'Everything Is Good For You' and 'Not the Girl You Think You Are', were released as singles in 1996. They were the three extra tracks that appeared on the *Recurring Dream* compilation album released in the same year. (See that album for more information on the tracks.)

7

Farewell to the World (2006)

Original VHS release:	December 1996
2-CD and 2-DVD editions release:	November 2006 (Parlophone and Capitol)
Personnel:	Neil Finn: vocals, guitar Nick Seymour: bass guitar, backing vocals Mark Hart: guitar, electric twelve-string guitar, keyboards, Hammond organ, melodica, Rhodes piano, backing vocals Paul Hester: drums, backing vocals Tim Finn: vocals and guitar ('Weather with You' and 'It's Only Natural' only) Peter Jones: drums ('Sister Madly') Jules Bowen: keyboards
Production:	Angus Davidson: sound design, live sound, DVD audio production Tchad Blake: audio mixing Noel Crombie: set/stage design
Duration:	106 minutes
Chart positions:	Australia: 46

As many Crowded House fans will tell you, in all their incarnations, the band have been the consummate live performers. *Farewell to the World* is a perfect summation of the live experience, and still to this day, the definitive live collection from the band. It is also acts as a good way of rounding off the first phase of the band.

The date of the gig was originally set for Saturday, 23 November 1996, but the weather put paid to that. The worst of the weather came on the Friday, but a decision was taken to move the gig to Sunday evening instead.

For the hundreds of fans who had flown to Australia for the chance to see their favourite band for one last time. Some fans would be travelling back on the day of the rearranged gig. To this end, they performed a soundcheck to 5,000 or so fans who had congregated at the venue. They did more than a rudimentary run-through of songs; while performing a portion of the set.

The band's farewell concert eventually went ahead on 24 November 1996 on the Sydney Opera House Forecourt at 5 pm. It was anticipated that 75,000 would turn out to see the band, but estimates have said that there may have been over 250,000 people in attendance.

The concert was originally aired on Network Ten in Australia in November 1996; however, this performance was incomplete as it did not include five songs (due to time constraints). On the DVD extras, Neil Finn said that some of the songs were omitted due to the odd fluff in the performances.

It is a genuinely emotional experience watching it even after all these years, especially when the band embraces at the end to a backdrop of fireworks.

Even with a massive crowd in front of them, like the many times they have played large venues over the years, they managed to make the gig seem intimate. The stage set felt quite small, in comparison to gigs of this scale today. There were not many screens appended to the stage, so they must have been dots in the distance at some points. It is good that the DVD and CD exist for those who were there.

It was a perfect showcase of their talents as a live band. It did seem a shame at the time that it was for the band. It is quite poignant seeing Paul Hester on top form as a drummer and raconteur.

The band's final concert was preserved for posterity with a live album and live DVD of their performance outside the Sydney Opera House by the Harbour Bridge on a balmy summer's night. It was the perfect farewell to the band.

Neil Finn was on guitar, ably assisted by Mark Hart, who added lead and slide guitar throughout the set. Keyboards and melodica, too.

There are many standouts from the set, with 'Private Universe' and its long jam being the best of the bunch. 'Four Seasons in One Day' was a perfect performance too.

'Hole in the River' is at its Doors-like best. The song was very atmospheric, given the settings and the time of night that they played. This became something of an extended jam too on the night.

For the encore, they were joined by Peter Jones, which allowed Paul Hester to come to the front of the stage and play stand-up drum on 'Sister Madly'. This included an impromptu version of 'Italian Plastic' that Hester nearly forgot the words to. On 'Weather With You', Tim Finn joined the band with a bit of call and response from the audience that became an elongated jam.

They played 'Throw Your Arms Around Me', a Hunters and Collectors cover, before ending with their biggest hit 'Don't Dream It's Over'.

The gig was originally released on VHS in December 1996, which included most of the television broadcast. Eventually, a fuller, more expansive version of the gig was released by Parlophone and Capitol in November 2006. This appeared in both two-CD and two-DVD editions. The DVD contained some extras, including a great commentary track and documentary extras.

Long-term associate Tchad Blake oversaw the 2006 audio remix. These releases also included the full set of songs for the first time. The DVDs have more of the in-between song banter and the antics that make for a typical Crowded House gig. The live CDs capture the same songs as the 24-song DVD, which concentrates on the songs without much of the in-between chatter.

Setlist

'Mean To Me', 'World Where You Live', 'When You Come', 'Private Universe', 'Four Seasons In One Day' 'Fall At Your Feet', 'Whispers And Moans', 'Hole In The River', 'Better Be Home Soon' 'Pineapple Head', 'Distant Sun', 'Into Temptation', 'Everything Is Good For You', 'Locked Out', 'Something So Strong', 'Sister Madly', 'Italian Plastic', 'Weather With You', 'It's Only Natural', 'There Goes God', 'Fingers Of Love', 'In My Command', 'Throw Your Arms Around Me', 'Don't Dream It's Over'

8

Time on Earth (2007)

Original album release:	June 2007
Deluxe Edition release:	November 2016
Personnel:	Neil Finn: vocals, guitars, Wurlitzer, piano and vibes Nick Seymour: bass, backing vocals and autoharp Mark Hart: piano, keyboards, electric guitar and harmonies (tracks 2, 3, 6 and 12) Matt Sherrod: drums (tracks 2, 3 and 12) and backing vocals (track 3) Ethan Johns: drums (tracks 1, 7, 9, 10, 11 and 13), backing vocals (track 1), harmony vocal (track 5), string arrangement (tracks S, 13 and 14), sitar (track 7), fuzz guitar, hurdy-gurdy (track 9) and guitar (track 11) Johnny Marr: electric guitar (tracks 2 and 6) and twelve-string acoustic guitar (track 6) Rikki Gooch: drums (tracks 4, 5 and 11), marching bass drum and cymbal (track 13) Elroy Finn: acoustic guitar (tracks 4, 5, 7 and 9) and electric guitar (track 11) Gavyn Wright: string leader (tracks S, 13 and 14) Isobel Griffiths: string contractor (tracks S, 13 and 14) Richard Watkins: French horn (track 5) Sonny Marr: backing vocal (track 6) Liam Finn: harmony vocal (tracks 7, 9 and 10) Eddie Raynor: piano idea (track 1) and harmonium (track 10) Sharon Finn: harmony (track 10) Don McGlashan: euphonium (track 10) and harmony (track 8)

	Beth Rowley: ethereal vocal (track 12, which appears courtesy of Blue Thumb Records, UCJ) Jay Joyce: guitar atmosphere (track 8) Joey Waronker: drums (track 14) Joseph Linsday, Isaac McNeill and Scott Towers: horns (track 7)
Recorded and produced by:	Ethan Johns at Roundhead Studios; except tracks 2, 3, 6 and 12, produced by Steve Lillywhite at RAK Studios, engineered by Jonathan Shakhovskoy, assistant engineer Helen Atkinson; track 14 produced by Neil Finn and Nick Seymour at Roundhead Studios, engineered by Ryan Freeland, assisted by Neil Baldock
Duration:	58:31
Chart positions:	Australia:1; New Zealand: 2; US: 46; UK: 3

The songs that formed *Time on Earth* were originally destined for Neil Finn's third solo album. While on tour with The Finn Brothers, the tragic news of Paul Hester's death emerged. A gig at the Royal Albert Hall in London brought about a Crowded House reunion of sorts as Nick Seymour flew from his home in Dublin to be with the brothers on stage to share a collective grief at the passing of their friend and former bandmate.

Neil Finn talked about the process of how the coming together happened:

> Nick and I reconnected, in the shadow of Paul's passing, and started hanging out quite a lot, and enjoying each other's company. And it was comforting, but it was also a rekindling of something. And, the natural thing was to play music again, together. And, you know, we started doing that, and at the end of last year, we had made this body of work, which felt to us like a band.[1]

The solo album that was taking shape included Nick Seymour on bass. He was there initially as a friend, not because of a Crowded House reunion. As the songs developed, Neil's thinking at the time was that he wanted it to be more of a band-led environment.

He was missing Hester, but also the chance to play with a band:

> Overall, I think Paul is a strong presence on the record, and it's not often really literal, but there is an underpinning of both sadness and reflection, and hopefully some degree of reverence and honour paid to him as well. It was a profound event in our lives and will always be deeply mysterious in a sense. We miss the little bugger, so yeah, he's all over the place.[2]

Some of the original demos were in great shape, but Ethan Johns wanted to start from scratch.

As Crowded House reassembled, they brought back multi-instrumentalist Mark Hart, who had joined the band full-time before the release of *Together Alone*. They rehearsed with numerous drummers across the world before they found Matt Sherrod. who had previously worked with Beck. He was chosen based on the likelihood of his bringing something new to the band and not replicating Hester's style. He was even encouraged to pick up other instruments when they got to record material.

Even though it was a Crowded House comeback album, several session musicians were employed in the initial stages of the recording process: Joey Waronker was on drums and the British singer Beth Rowley, provided the vocals for 'Transit Lounge'. Johnny Marr played and co-wrote a song with Neil on 'Even a Child'.

Nick Seymour, Mark Hart and Matt Sherrod only performed on four tracks, which include 'Don't Stop Now', the album's lead single and 'She Called Up'. In addition to the tunes that existed for the planned solo album, the reconstituted Crowded House wrote several tunes that would complete the album.

It is an album that looks forward, while also noting the passing of time.

Despite his death, Paul Hester is at the forefront of the thoughts of the principal songwriter, Neil Finn:

> I had a song called 'Time on Earth' which went through a transition and ended up not being a song that made the grade, but the song title just came back to me when we were examining our state of mind, probably in the shadow of Paul [Hester]'s passing to some degree, but also as we get older. The idea that we have a transitory state we're in, and that you have to be here. There's a lot of very simple and eloquent philosophy based on the principle of being where you are in the moment, and I think it is just another way of evoking that idea and as a band, so no time like now to inhabit this earth.[3]

The original album was produced by Ethan Johns, except for 'Don't Stop Now', 'She Called Up', 'Even A Child' and 'Transit Lounge', which were produced by Steve Lillywhite, who finally got the chance to work with the band after being overlooked for the *Together Alone* sessions. 'People Are Like Suns' was produced by Neil Finn and Nick Seymour.

Nick Seymour, as ever, was responsible for the artwork of the album, which was his first attempt at collage assemblage depicting agoraphobia:

> Don't leave the house; you may be overwhelmed and consumed. The newspaper towers represent the ever-present news media doom narrative. Giotto's 'Tree of Life' offers slender solace, but the castaway is ultimately plucked and taken by the monster of the deep.[4]

Time on Earth was originally released in June 2007 on Parlophone & ATO Records. A deluxe edition was released in November 2016.

The sleeve notes include a dedication to their former drummer, which reads 'In Memory of Paul Hester.'

The tracks

'Nobody Wants To'

Written by Neil Finn
Duration: 4:10

There is something pastoral about the opening bars of the songs of the opening number of *Time on Earth*. It is a song that would not have sounded out of place on either of The Finn Brothers' albums.

The delicately strummed acoustic guitars. The low rumble of Nick Seymour's bass makes its presence known as the song unfolds. There is a certain wistfulness about the music. Lyrically, the song is about the words left unsaid and people's inability to find the right words, and how Neil Finn wants them to be said: 'I'm attracted to raking them up and, once exposed, they're often less dangerous somehow, or less threatening.'[5]

It has one of those Crowded House melodies that slowly creeps up on you.

It unmistakably sounds like a Crowded House number, even though it was initially planned as one of the tracks for the solo album. It is a more mature take on what a Crowded House song should be. The chorus is subtle and effective. This song alone more than justifies the band's return.

'Don't Stop Now'

Written by Neil Finn
Duration: 3:54
Released as a single in June 2007

The first single from the band in eleven years, and the first to be released from the album. It is a family drama set to music and played out in under four minutes.

Neil Finn has form in turning things that have happened at home into hit material. Having decamped to England to live near Bath in 2006, Finn's wife, Sharon, decided to go for a drive down the country lanes of England. However, the conditions and her unfamiliarity with the area made the journey all the more challenging, as Neil Finn explained:

> It descended into an incredibly dark and stormy night, as the song says. She got lost and rang me a bit distressed. I had to guide her in and, after I'd got her back to the house and she'd calmed down, I played her the song I'd been writing and said all I was lacking was a title, and she came up with the title.[6]

Johnny Marr gets to add his trademark guitar lines to this one. He has been a notable guest star on many a live outing for Neil Finn and the band down the years; it is great to hear him on a Crowded House record at last.

The guitar riff that runs through the song is quite catchy. The piano stabs add to the tension and the tempestuous lyrical edge of the song. New drummer, Matt Sharrod, makes his presence known with a pounding rhythm that drives the song along. The middle eight ramps up the tension quite effectively, with the discordant piano helping to show the tension.

The home demo that appears on the deluxe edition captures the essence of the track that ended up on the album. The verses highlight the inspiration of trying to offer directions for someone who is lost. The mention of the Rose and Crown pub in the demo is changed to the more figurative 'Is the devil gonna track me down' in the final version.

The single, which announced the band's return, was released on 16 June 2007 in the UK and Australia in numerous formats and variations to the tracklists. The versions contain new songs 'Lost Island' and 'Stare Me Out' (both songs can be found on the 2016 Deluxe Edition of the album), as well as versions of 'Heaven That I'm Making' and 'Mean to Me' from a RealWorld Sessions Webcast. A UK Enhanced CD edition was released with a video of the single. The video is largely animated, replicating elements of the album's cover art.

'She Called Up'

Written by Neil Finn
Duration: 2:53
Released as a single in September 2007

There is an air of melancholy that hangs over the lyrical content of the album. This is inevitable given the passing of Paul Hester. This song is a case in point. It could be read into the lyrics that it is about a romantic entanglement that has run its course, while in reality, it is a song about the emotions of hearing the news that someone close has died.

Musically, it is upbeat and has the hallmarks of a classic Crowded House single. In some quarters, reviews have even said the style is reminiscent of Split Enz. The cheerful nature of the song does belie the fact that this is a reflection on the passing of the band's friend and former drummer. The 'la-la' refrain is unmistakably poppy. The jaunty keyboard part throughout adds to the upbeat nature of the song. The chorus begs to be sung along with.

There is an interesting demo version that is more laid-back and what Neil Finn describes as an 'ignorant New Zealander's version of reggae.'[7] Finn likes the rough edges of that version and has questioned whether the final version was better.

It was released as a single in September 2007, backed with 'So Dramatic', 'People Are Like Suns' (piano version) and a video of the single.

'Say That Again'

Written by Neil Finn
Duration: 5:21

Another song earmarked for the solo album, and it is one of the longer songs on the album.

Lyrically, the song went through several stages before it ended up with this finished version, as Neil Finn has noted:

> This one had lyrics that never ended up being in the song, which was about the idea of a ship coming close to you and the distance between, trying to work out how far something is away on the ocean. Apart from that, it's just about words. The idea that the person that you love or your muse—the girl that sits on the shore and combs her hair—gives you the inspiration to have courage and be a man. The little things that come along that lodge in your head to make you see things differently and abandon your plan.[8]

It has a laid-back feel to it. The guitars and rhythm pattern tick along effectively. There is an intricate guitar line that gives the song its dreamlike quality. It contains one of the earliest contributions from Elroy Finn on acoustic guitar; there will be more from him in due course.

'Pour Le Monde'

Written by Neil Finn
Duration: 5:11
Released as a single in June 2007

This is a big, bold, piano-led song. The vocals from Finn are amongst the best he has recorded in his career. There is minimal backing on this one. Neil's son Elroy adds some acoustic guitar.

The drums are from Rikki Gooch—he is one of four drummers credited on the album. That shows the diversity of talent on *Time on Earth*. His contribution to this track fits in with the feel and the swing of the song. It would have been up there as one of the best Neil Finn solo tracks if it had been released as originally planned. As a Crowded House song, it certainly can hold its own amongst all the other great tracks the band have released down the years. There are excellent harmonies in the bridge and the outro.

The second phase of Crowded House has been blessed with three great singles so far. It is a close call, but this is certainly up there as being the best of that set. When interviewed before the release of the album, Nick Seymour said that the song 'stands for nobility and integrity'.

Neil Finn was inspired by events that led up to the Iraq War:

> I was partially inspired for the song by seeing a demonstration march in Paris against the war at the time. France was keeping out of it, but there was a lot of activity. This song, as a lot of them are, comes from different strands of thought that seem to have a connection with each other, one of them being the idea of people being tortured and lifting—going out of their bodies.[9]

In early studio recordings of the song, titled 'C'est Ne Pas Un Chien' ['It's Not a Dog']. The first two verses of that song were sung in French. Incidentally, 'Pour la Monde' means 'For the World' in French.

The third single from the album and it came with extra tracks across different formats, including 'Something So Strong' and 'You Are the One to Make Me Cry', both recorded live in North America. The iTunes exclusive bundle comes with an additional version of the song played live at the iTunes Festival.

'Even A Child'

Written by Neil Finn and Johnny Marr
Duration: 3:58

Johnny Marr has been a regular associate of Neil Finn over the years. There is the 8 Worlds collaboration. There is also the agreement of joining each other's respective bands for occasional guest spots when on respective tours. This is the first time the pair shared a co-write on a Crowded House song.

The song has the Marr's trademark jangly arpeggiated guitar throughout. The strummed guitar gives the song that upbeat and summery feel. There is a jagged guitar line which helps it avoid being too saccharine. The bassline is understated but drives the song along. The Finn vocals are in the higher register and help to further project the summery nature of the song. It is quite a poppy song, and it must have been in the running to be one of the singles.

It is a song about not wasting time and remembering what is important in life. It is a song that was written for the solo album, and with the passing of Paul Hester, although it is not about him, the sentiment of not wasting time shines through, as Neil Finn has noted:

> I wrote this song with Johnny Marr at the beach in New Zealand, and that phrase was quite a difficult one to work out because it's what came out accidentally. I couldn't quite rationalise how that fitted together, and then finally, a few pennies dropped, and the chorus came, and at the same time, he did a demo at home. He had his daughter, Sonny, singing on it, and she is still, in fact, on the track, although there are other voices in there. There was something about the sound of her sweet voice that reminded me that certain truths are known by children and forgotten by adults quite regularly. When you get given a present or a gift or anything, you don't waste it.[10]

'Heaven That I'm Making'

Written by Neil Finn
Duration: 3:56

It was a stylistically diverse album and it would be hard to second-guess what comes next when listening to it for the first time.

This one has a groove inspired by the drummer Joey Waronker, who initially played on the song. It is not his version that appears on the record; that is attributed to Ethan Jones, who produced several tracks on the album.

The track is in 6/8 time, which gives it a distinct feel. It is a mellow and contemplative song in the verses that builds to the chorus. There is what sounds like a Fender Rhodes in the mix, which ramps up in the chorus and the extended instrumental section. This, along with the groove of the song, acts as the hook.

Some of the instrumentation in the intro evokes memories of the *Together Alone* album. The acoustic guitars, drums and vocals at the end do not so much fade out but resolve the song and the thoughts running through the lyrics. The melody line sounds unmistakably Crowded House, but the overall feel is something else.

The lyrics are meditative and symbolic, but not in an overtly religious way. It is almost the idea of creating a heaven, or a haven in your own space.

'A Sigh'

Written by Neil Finn
Duration: 3:17

There is something elegiac and ethereal about 'A Sigh'. An evocative opening gives way to softly strummed guitars. The effects on the guitars sound cavernous, and link well with the line 'deepest well'. There is a faint church organ in the background that adds to the mood of the song. There are the faint echoes of a choir as the song fades out.

There is a self-admitted vulnerability in Neil Finn's vocals and the lyrical content:

> I'm always searching for the two parallel worlds in one lyric, where there's something in the here and now that's very physical and grounded. There's another thing which is to do with yearnings and little stirrings in the back of your brain that you don't quite understand. In a literal sense, a sigh conjures up a lot, and there are lots of different ways that you can sigh, and it tells a lot, as the opening line suggests. In terms of grappling with some of the things that have come up in the last couple of years, that's all I was left with, and all I was trying to evoke is the feeling of the unspoken being immense.[11]

The song acts as a moment of calm and peace in the middle of the album. There are not a lot of lyrics (or verses on this one), but they say a lot about Finn's mindset in that period.

'Silent House'

Written by Neil Finn, Emily Robison, Martie Maguire and Natalie Maines
Duration: 5:52

At first glance, the title could be seen as alluding to Paul Hester's passing. The inspiration for the song comes from another source. Freed from being in Crowded House, Neil Finn involved himself with some interesting collaborations during his solo years. This one comes from that time, and the opportunity arose from an invitation to co-write with Natalie Maines, from The Chicks (formerly The Dixie Chicks). He explained how the song and the collaboration evolved:

> We had breakfast one morning, and I can honestly say I didn't know more than one or two songs of theirs, but I loved their political stance. I thought it was brilliant that they were unapologetic and didn't back down, and I knew they were great singers. It was intriguing, and we sat down for two or three days and came up with this song. It's something I've very rarely done, but it's good for you. It's quite challenging, though. Confronting. Because my approach is so random, I feel I'm slightly an impostor when I sit down in a room full of people.[12]

There is a build to the chorus in the verse, with a fuzz-tone effect on the guitar. The arrangement explodes with the chorus. The combined vocal talents of Neil Finn and The Chicks work well to add a tenderness to the jagged musical arrangement. There is a great, extended, atmospheric instrumental coda where the band let loose. It sounds like one of those great Neil Young solos that seem to be falling apart but somehow stay on track to drive the song along. There is a repetitive, mantra-like appeal to the song.

Lyrically, this song comes from the experiences of Nathalie Maines and her grandmother Nonna's Alzheimer's:

> It just seems like the worst way to end your life, when you can't remember any of it. But she touched a lot of people, and we all remember. So, this song is about that: It's okay to forget, I'll try and carry on.[13]

She also described the song as being 'a sad song that tries to be sweet'.[14]

'English Trees'

Written by Neil Finn
Duration: 3:43

The song is reflective of Neil Finn's time living in England, and the death of Paul Hester hangs heavy over this one. Although he is not mentioned by name, there are references to his passing, for instance, 'In Regent's Park I will mourn for you and I must be wise somehow because my heart's been broken down.'[15]

It is another thoughtful and emotional number on the album. Neil Finn's vocals sound like they are struggling with the emotion of the song. It is another reflection on the seasons from Finn:

> In England, the seasons are very clearly marked, and they also, to some degree, are a constant reflection on the moods of men and women and the passing of time, and that's what I was reflecting on. There must be something that you can understand or something that you can grasp hold of that gives you a clue as to life in tragic circumstances, but you can't see it at the time.[16]

There is a beautifully melancholic melody to the song, with the family Finn helping with the backing vocals, with Neil's wife Sharon and Liam added to the mix. Don McGlashan plays euphonium on the track, which sits in the background excellently. The England that Finn conjures up with lyrics is enhanced by the evocative sounds used on the track.

'Walked Her Way Down'

Written by Neil Finn
Duration: 4:17

This opens up as another piano-led number, but the band comes in as the song progresses with a more expansive arrangement. After a run of slow-building and emotional songs, this is a more up-tempo number. There are some great sonic textures. With the piano shaping the song's direction.

It is another of the solo songs that have been repurposed for the Crowded House album. The lyrics evoke the theme of the album, although a track called 'Time on Earth' never cut for the album. 'Walked Her Way Down', which could act as the thematic summation of the album, 'is about recognising our time on Earth,' said Neil Finn, 'as being something you have to grab by the throat and be aware of all the time'.[17]

'Transit Lounge'

Written by Neil Finn
Duration: 4:26

Given the international success of Neil Finn and Crowded House, this is a reflection on those times spent in departure lounges of airports in exotic far-off places. Attracting all walks of life, not just pop stars. Transient place with incongruously named bars like the Coconut Grove mentioned in the song are manna from heaven for an ever-observant songwriter like Neil Finn.

Another transient figure adds a lovely, haunting, ethereal vocal on the track. While the album was being recorded at RAK Studios, Beth Rowley was there working on another project and ended up contributing to this track. The vocals have that soaring quality to them reminiscent of Clare Torry on Pink Floyd's 'Great Gig in the Sky'.

The instrumentation does evoke the sights and sounds of the departure lounge. The twisty bass at the start and throughout was not from the usual source. Nick Seymour was happy to let someone else take care of the bass on this track.

> 'Matt came up with that bass line in the uplifting section where you've got those announcements—he sang it to me. The bass does this fantastic climb through these notes. It was Matt Sherrod's genius. I was delighted with that.[18]

The song includes keyboards from Mark Hart and production from Steve Lillywhite. This is a song that was written as a Crowded House number and not for the planned solo project.

'You Are the One to Make Me Cry'

Written by Neil Finn
Duration: 3:43

This is another brittle and haunting song that has the same melancholic edge that pervades the album as a whole. The strings and the vocal stylings allied with sombre keyboard sounds give the song a timeless quality.

The lyrics were inspired by a book that Finn had read about Robert Hewitt, the brother of New Zealand rugby player Norm Hewitt. The filmic quality of the music makes it ideal for a soundtrack, were a film of the events ever to be made.

Neil Finn recounts the story of Hewitt and the inspirations for the song:

> He was lost at sea for two-and-a-half days, floating in his wetsuit with just a bag of these things called kina, which are seafood. He stayed alive in a freezing cold ocean and was eventually plucked from the ocean and saved at a point where nobody gave him even a half a chance because it was way longer than he was supposed to have lived—to the point where some people thought it was a setup. He described, in the paper, his hallucinations that he had, as he was getting on to the second night, of sitting around the table with his family and his friends and how the image of his wife was what kept him sustained.[19]

The music was something that had been knocking around for a while, but the lyrical inspirations of the story seemed to fit in well with the type of song Finn wanted to write.

'People Are Like Suns'

Written by Neil Finn
Duration: 3:53

This is another piano arrangement and adds to the emotionally-charged outro of the album's last two tracks. Neil Finn has said that the song was inspired by Ian McEwan's 2005 novel *Saturday*: 'There's a scene at the beginning of that book where the guy's out on the balcony in London, looking out at the night sky. This song was set in my mind in that urban environment.'[20]

This is another beautifully arranged song. There's an even more tender version of the song, with its beautifully brittle arrangement on the deluxe edition of the album. It's also an extra track on the 'She Called Up' single. The song's vulnerability is yet again reinforced by Finn's tender vocals, more so on this version, with the stripped-back guitar tracks.

2016 Deluxe Edition bonus disc (Lester Records & Kobalt)

'She Called Up' (home demo), 'A Sigh' (home demo), 'Here's A Note' (studio demo),
'Purple Light' (studio demo), 'So Dramatic', 'Stare Me Out' (alternative version), 'Distance Across' (studio demo), 'Lost Island', 'Stare Me Out', 'Bound to Rescue'(home demo) 'Don't Stop Now' (home demo), 'Won't Be Silent' (home demo), 'People Are Like Suns' (piano version)

Again, the band has released an expanded edition of the album featuring several demo versions of songs that made the album, as well as a few that were in the running for the album but missed out. Given the original album's fourteen-track running order, these inevitably were left on the sidelines. In some territories and formats, some of the extras appeared on the alternate editions of the main album; for instance, the tracks 'Lost Island' and 'Stare Me Out' are available on the vinyl version of this album.

The tracks

'Here's A Note' (studio demo)

Written by Neil Finn
Duration: 2:27

This is a guitar-heavy number that is very much in its infancy. Maybe it did not fit sonically with the original album, which was at times quite introspective. The lyrics are inspired by Neil's Dad, who used to keep notes about everything related to his son's career: 'He'll write a little note, or he'll cut a bit of the newspaper out to remind him of something, and then he'll put piles around the house.'[21]

'Purple Light' (studio demo)

Written by Neil Finn
Duration: 4:40

This started life as 'Time on Earth', the inspiration for the title of the album. It was first recorded for the *One All* sessions back in 2001. There is a jaunty melody and a great guitar riff that runs through this one. The coda is hooky enough to consider this as another great song that got away. It was recorded many times by Finn to get it right, but it just did not quite land.

It was one that people around the band liked. Perceptibly, they did envisage where it would end up, as Jeremy Ansell, Crowded House associate, reflected in the notes of the deluxe edition: 'I was there one of the nights when you did a take, and I thought, 'I love that song!' You were saying already then that you didn't think it would be on the album, but maybe in ten years you could release it on some box set.'[22]

Finally, it did land on disc two of the deluxe edition.

'So Dramatic'

Written by Neil Finn
Duration: 3:36

Another piano-led number that sounds like it might be from a film soundtrack, it is another one that languishes in that extra track, missing B-side void.

The process of writing albums had become complicated over time. It was not just about the main album, with the need for hits. It was also about the extras and incentives to entice the diehard fans. This is something that Neil Finn has felt that the record companies have pushed to the limit:

> 'There are all sorts of reasons that record companies give you for needing a bonus track and It is just as bad now as it ever was 'cause you have to give a bonus track to iTunes, you have to give a bonus track to Pandora, you used to have to have one for Japan. It was a pain in the arse. I always felt it was exploitative. You're trying to get your hardcore fans to buy as many versions as you possibly could.[23]

'Stare Me Out' (Alternate Version)

Duration: 3:27
Written by Neil Finn

'Stare Me Out' (B-side version)

Duration: 4:16
Written by Neil Finn

The guitar riff at the start sounds like it is about to evolve into David Bowie's 'Heroes'. The guitar line, is reminiscent of Robert Fripp, and acts as a brilliant

Above: The Classic Line Up: The New Zealand rock group Crowded House at the Montreux Festival in 1987. From left: Paul Hester, Nick Seymour, Neil Finn. (*Alamy stock photo*)

Below: Liam Mullane Finn, son of Neil Finn, performs live on stage at the Isle of Wight Festival, 21 June 2024. (*SOPA Images Limited/Alamy Live News*)

Above: Neil Finn performing live on stage at the Salford Lowry, Manchester, 27 April 2014. (*Alamy stock photo*)

Below: Neil and Tim performing as The Finn Brothers. (*Alamy stock photo*)

Above: Neil Finn performing live in Brighton, October 2024. (*Alamy stock photo*)

Right: The Finn Brothers—Neil (left) and Tim Finn—during an in-store appearance at Virgin Megastore on Oxford Street, central London, signing copies of their new single 'Won't Give In', from the album *Everyone Is Here*. This was their first collaboration since Crowded House split in 1996. (*Alamy stock photo*)

Above: Crowded House Mark II, photographed in Bristol on the Thekla Social boat, 19 March 2007. Left to right: Neil Finn, Matt Sherrod, Nick Seymour and Mark Hart. (*Alamy stock photo*)

Below: Elroy Finn performs live on stage at Isle of Wight Festival, 21 June 2024. (*Alamy stock photo*)

Above: The band performing in front of a packed audience at the 2024 Eden Sessions. (*Alamy stock photo*)

Below: Neil Finn (left) and his son Liam playing live at Scarborough Open Air Theatre, 11 June 2022. (*Ernesto Rogata/Alamy Live*)

John McVie, Mick Fleetwood, Mike Campbell, Stevie Nicks, Christine McVie and Neil Finn of Fleetwood Mac arrive for the iHeartRadio Music Festival at the T-Mobile Arena in Las Vegas, Nevada, on 21 September 2018. (*James Atoa/UPI/Alamy*)

Nick Seymour, bassist and original member. (*Alamy stock photo*)

Above: Neil Finn performs a headlining gig at Glasgow Royal Concert Hall, 23 April 2014. (*Alamy stock photo*)

Below: Promotional photo from 1987. Left to right: Neil Finn, Nick Seymour and Paul Hester. (*Dennis Keeley/Alamy stock photo*)

Neil and Elroy Finn as Red Bull Racing guests at the Formula 1 World Championship in Singapore, 5 October 2025. (*James Moy/Alamy Live News*)

Neil Finn performs at Rod Laver Arena, Melbourne, on 10 December 2024. (*Alamy stock photo*)

hook. It also marks one of the first contributions from Elroy Finn for the band.

Neil Finn had a proud-dad moment, as he noted on the Crowded House Club newsletter in 2007:

> That song is Elroy's debut as an electric guitarist, and in fact, that very prominent solo on there is the very first played in his life. He did it on the floor, live with the rhythm track and added a little bit afterwards, so it means a lot to me, that moment. It's an explosive moment where he proved that he's got a bit of latent Hendrix genealogy in there somewhere. It's high energy.[24]

It appears on the 'Don't Stop Now' single in its original form. That, too, appears on the deluxe edition.

The lyrics are inspired by a praying mantis that perched itself on top of a piano, as Neil Finn recounts on the deluxe edition box set:

> I was doing a tour with Bic Runga in New Zealand, playing piano, which is an enjoyable outing for a musician. We were playing in a vineyard in Nelson, outdoors. I had a little upright piano and while Bic was playing one of her songs, a praying mantis came walking down the top of the piano and stopped right in front of me, turned around, got up on its hind legs and looked me in the eye—I swear—and started swaying its head side to side in rhythm with the music. [25]

The version that appears on the B-side tones down the 'Heroes'-style guitar. The brass section is pushed higher up in the mix. The guitar riff is more staccato on this one.

'Distance Across' (studio demo)

Written by Neil Finn
Duration: 3:15

A carefree number that evolved into the more laid-back 'Say That Again'. In the form that it appears on the deluxe edition, it is incomplete and includes guide notes in the song to how it should be completed.

'Lost Island'

Written by Neil Finn
Duration: 4:16

This one feels like a not-too-distant cousin of 'Kare Kare' in tone a song from *Together Alone* in the way it was recorded.

It is one that Neil is fond of as he told his listeners on the *Fangradio* Christmas Special in December 2020:

> One of my favourites. It's a West Coast (New Zealand) song, looking at Lion Rock, watching the sun disappear into the little mouth at the end of the rock, full of dreams and possibilities.[26]

In the *Fangradio* special about *Time on Earth,* Neil Finn said this should have been on the album proper and not just as a bonus track for those who purchased the vinyl edition.

They had a Welsh choir come in for the recording when the Finns lived in the church house, just outside Bath. The choir came in and recorded their part in a moment that recalls how the song 'Together Alone' came together.

This is not to be confused with 'To the Island', which appears on the *Dreamers Are Waiting* album released in 2021.

'Bound To Rescue' (home demo)

Written by Neil Finn
Duration: 2:31

This was another demo that was recorded in the Church House in Bath. It is another minimalistic piano number from Finn. There are assorted backing vocals, which show the potential of the song.

This was tried in many forms, as Neil Finn has noted: 'We did a version of it at Leigh Sawmill, which was pretty good as well. Some of them rise and some of them do not.'[27]

It did rise eventually when Finn played it on one of his early sessions on the *Fangradio* broadcasts in April 2020.

'Won't Be Silent' (home demo)

Written by Neil Finn and Nick Seymour
Duration: 3:35

It is ostensibly a Nick Seymour song that was put forward for the album, but it was too late to make it. It has been given an outing eventually on the deluxe edition. It was recorded and mixed by Nick Seymour in Sligo in 2006. It stems from trying to articulate what he wanted from the song he was writing.

In the notes for the album, he explained his reasoning:

> When we were in the studio, I tried to impose a direction for it that would be a more Motown idea of rendering it in a Reverend Al Green way, and I just didn't make my articulations clear enough. So, I felt, to get the idea across, I'd better actually do a demo.[28]

It features him on lead vocals and has an electric piano and drum machine backing.

9

Intriguer (2010)

Original album released in June 2010 (Universal & Fantasy)
Deluxe Edition released in November 2016(Universal)

Personnel:	Neil Finn: vocals, guitars, keyboards and piano Nick Seymour: bass Mark Hart: guitars and piano Matt Sherrod: drums Don McGlashan: mandolin, tambourine, acoustic and electric guitar and euphonium Sharon Finn: vocals Liam Finn: electric guitar on 'Isolation' Lisa Germano: violin on 'Archer's Arrows' and 'Even If' Jon Brion:guitar and vocals on 'Twice If You're Lucky' Jim Scott: low piano, tambourine, shaker and sleigh bell Michael McClintock: violin on 'Even If' Greg Leisz: pedal steel guitar on 'Elephants'
Recorded at:	Roundhead Studios, Auckland, May-August 2009
Duration:	40:19
Produced by:	Jim Scott and Neil Finn
Chart positions:	Australia: 1; New Zealand: 3; UK: 12; US: 50

For Neil Finn, the album is a sign of the band moving forward. The band had attempted to do something that was a little less polished, and in contrast to the last album, it was hoped that they could create something that sounded like a band playing together in the room. Nick Seymour thinks the album is 'underbaked, but that's a good thing. We knew it was time to stop at a certain point. That's a good sign.'[1]

The album was produced by Jim Scott and Neil Finn mainly at Roundhead Studios, Auckland, between May and August 2009, with some additional recording at Exchequer Studios, Dublin.

The title, *Intriguer,* derives from an observation of Neil Finn's:

> He's a character that Michael Leunig and I invented and enjoyed from being in a hotel lobby in Sydney and observing some intriguing behaviour behind a curtain on the seventh floor. The Intriguer is the designer of unexpected events. You never really see him close up; you just see a shadowy figure in the background.[2]

It is a lean album with ten tracks in total. It is the shortest collection of the band's career. About twenty-five songs were in the running at some point; that was the number that was presented to Jim Scott when he was invited to produce the album. It is the last of the albums to have been given a deluxe edition release. This expands the collection by an additional sixteen tracks. Songs that did not quite make it, extra tracks on digital releases, or are alternate/demo versions.

The original album was released on 11 June 2010. A deluxe edition followed in November 2016. It is an album that, at the time of release, seemed to be well-received by critics and fans around the world. In episode six of the *Fangradio* broadcast on 29 April 2020, Neil Finn performed 'Other Side of the World'. He alluded to the fact that he felt this album had been somewhat overlooked at the time.

The artwork for the album was again produced by Nick Seymour:

> I tried many ways of rendering the randomness of urban poster art, degenerating from weather, defaced by graffitists and scribes. Short of painting something and leaving it for a few weeks on a street corner, I composed this work entirely on a computer, juxtaposing Matt's wife Kelly's comforting Teddy Child Light with a would-be stencilled font with stitched buttons on builders' ply with the Intriguer lettering scribed by a passer-by... A depiction of installation, process and integrity.[3]

The tracks

'Saturday Sun'

Written by Neil Finn
Duration: 3:26
Released as a single in April 2010

It is the percussion section that is to the forefront on the band's first single from the album.

Nick Seymour gets the album off to a flying start with a thick bassline that highlights the desire to shake up the sound on this album. The bass and drums are quite the hook.

Sonically, the verse sounds like a shift in style for the band. Their noted organic sounds that they are famed for have been replaced by a more distinct electronic edge. The digital release has more of the electronic hum in the extra seconds of the intro. That texture can be heard in the background throughout the song. The vocal sound is also given an electronic treatment.

Neil Finn explained some of the experiments:

> I got given a micro KORG synthesiser/vocoder by Jon Brion while we were recording in L.A. with Jim Scott. He came out and did a couple of overdubs, and he gave it to me, and I put it to work straight away on that song. It helped us to see it into a different sonic landscape.[4]

The chorus is unmistakably Crowded House, despite the experimentations. It is a bold start to the album. It is certainly up there with some of the great Crowded House singles.

There is a more straightforward version of the song that appears on the deluxe box set, stripped of the electronic elements. It had potential and a lightness of touch, but the finished, final version highlights how the experiment pays off. There is a different middle eight on the demo, too. This was replaced with the far better one for the final release.

As is the modern way, it was released as a digital single, with no extra tracks. The video for the single was directed by Simon and Dominic Taylor, reflects the different stylings of the song. It looks like the band in a negative composition, playing live and sitting around by the swimming pool. The effects render the band to look like The Blue Man Group. The aesthetics fit in with the electronic style of the song.

'Archer's Arrows'

Written by Neil Finn
Duration: 4:05

The rhythm section is quite prominent again, with the martial drum pattern leading the way to something again that is electronic and experimental. The keyboard pattern sounds quite childlike, and the first lyrics of the song link well to the naïve nature of the song.

Sharon Finn lends her vocals to the chorus; this is more prominent than to describe it as a backing vocal. This is a nice counterpoint to Neil's distinctive vocals. Those who have heard the Pajama Club's album would be familiar with this set-up and Sharon's vocals. The band are augmented by Lisa Germano on violin, someone Neil Finn collaborated with to good effect previously on the 7 Worlds Collide project.

Again, the chorus is a refuge for those looking for something more familiar from a Crowded House song. Neil Finn is signing energetically, a nice counterpoint to Sharon's vocals.

Lyrically, it is another song inspired by time marching on and inspired by a movie that Finn had watched: 'It is a metaphor: lofty ambitions and your aim suddenly falls short. In a Chinese movie, *Hero*, there's a tremendous scene with thousands of arrows going into the air, and I'd seen that the day before.'[5]

A faster tempo version of the song can be heard on the deluxe edition of the album. This one is more organic, with different lyrics. Finn is describing his studio room at home, including another reference to Neil Finn's beloved dog, Lester.

'Amsterdam'

Written by Neil Finn
Duration: 3:35

The vocals come in at the first bar with a sample and drums. After the experimental sound of the opening numbers, this is a mid-tempo guitar-led number. It does open with an old-style record as a sample. Neil's Optigan is used to good effect on this one. The structure is atypical for the band, especially as it does not include the tried-and-tested musical intro. Neil Finn starts signing from the opening beat of the drum. It is a song that features the regular band and no guests.

Lyrically, the song is a travelogue that explores a trip to Amsterdam. It takes in the cultural delights of the city, Vincent Van Gogh and political protests. It paints a vivid picture of the sights of the city.

'Either Side of The World'

Written by Neil Finn
Duration: 4:35

There is something tranquil and exotic about the sound of this one. Another interesting rhythm pattern opens up this one. The pattern is reminiscent of the Fred Neil song 'Everybody's Talkin''. It has a backing track that sounds very summery. There is a vulnerability in the vocals.

The lyrical content seems to echo the tranquillity of the song. 'Getting away' is the lyrical theme. The build to the chorus, where the song gets louder, gives way to a woozy, dreamy section. You could be forgiven for thinking that the song is over at the three-minute mark, just before the piano and cymbals reignite the song for an extended break before the chorus comes back in. The catchy piano run underneath the chorus locks in with the percussion to good effect.

'Falling Dove'

Written by Neil Finn
Duration: 4:35

A delicately strummed number. The songs on the album, so far, have been predominantly about the percussion section; this one is more about the vocals, guitar and piano, the former again tender and dreamlike.

It opens as a mellow song, the verses wistful and tender. Then the chorus ignites the song with a build at the end that sounds very Beatlesque. This part of the song creeps up on you. The twistiness of the arrangement invokes a journey, something that comes through in the lyrics. Neil Finn explained what the inspiration to where the song came from:

> The music had been around for a little while. It seemed to be suitable for a mysterious journey through the Russian countryside on the midnight train from Moscow to St Petersburg. That idea of a journey mixed in with all those images and impressions from the intriguing Russian spy novels that I read when I was younger.[6]

The arrangement seems to cram a lot into its four-minute-thirty-five-seconds runtime. It feels longer, but in a good way. It seems to be one of the songs that gets overlooked in the Crowded House back catalogue, but certainly worth checking out. It is a wonderfully underrated number that sits well in the middle of the album.

'Isolation'

Written by Neil Finn, Nick Seymour, Mark Hart and Matt Sherrod
Duration: 4:38

So far, the album has been predominantly written by Neil Finn. This one is a co-write from the band that evolved from a jam.

There are two versions of the song that exist across the deluxe edition. The album version is markedly different to the demo track. The original is more folky and lacks the female vocals. The lyrics are significantly changed across the versions, too. There is a more prominent slide guitar that gives that version a more countrified feel.

The version that was released on the original album has a different tone altogether. The arpeggiated guitar acts as a hook to the song. It is another one of those numbers on the album that creeps up on you with repeated listens. The coda has an extended guitar workout that shows the band locked in to good effect. The male-female counterpoint works well in this version. The female vocals come from Sharon Finn.

Neil Finn explained in the *Crowded House Club* newsletter at the time of the release of the album: 'Sharon has an innocent approach in a sense that it's not affected; her voice isn't mannered or stylised; it's just a lovely tone, beautiful, simple, honest singing which I like, and it suited the song "Isolation". She can sound breathy and ethereal, so it worked out well.'[7]

Like many songs throughout their career, the band has played unreleased tracks at gigs to road test them and, at times, to reshape them in the live arena.

This can be both a good and a bad thing, as Neil Finn noted in the notes for the deluxe edition:

> People get attached to the way that they are. They heard them the first time, and so there were certain songs that we did on those tours that ended up quite different, you know, and immensely preferred the new versions, but people had bootleg versions of what we did on stage, and so there was a bit of discontent here and there about the way that songs had been ruined for certain people.[8]

It is one that Neil Finn played a few times on his *Fangradio* broadcasts in a stripped-back form.

'Twice If You're Lucky'

Written by Neil Finn
Duration: 3:33

The piano arrangement opens the song and then pushes it along, with a low-key slide guitar deployed successfully. It is another song that the band had played live before it was released on an album.

A live version can be heard on the deluxe edition. It shows the evolution of the song and it again highlights Neil Finn's ability to turn something that might be okay, into something that finds its way to being a very good song:

> We played it live, and I thought it was too simple, and I discovered this whole other verse section that made it a much more complex song, and I thought a more substantial song. We recorded it a few times in that way, but I still felt that we hadn't nailed it. Then I took it back to the simple form that it had at the very beginning, and it is now way better for it.[9]

It has one of those subtle melodies that gets under your skin after repeated plays.

'Inside Out'

Written by Neil Finn
Duration: 3:19

A regulation guitar rocker that bounces along quite well. The usual band members were augmented by Don McGlashan on electric guitar. He is usually heard providing the more exotic instruments on Crowded House albums. The stripped-back nature of the song sounds like the band were having a good time recording this one. This is evidenced by the wailing guitars and the extended jam at the end of the song.

'Even If'

Written by Neil Finn
Duration: 4:04

The melody is present on the demo version, which appears on the deluxe edition, highlighting the evolution of the song. You can hear Neil Finn strumming the initial chords of the song on the guitar. He instructs Mark Hart to play a potential idea for a piano line. There is some instruction towards the end about how the percussion track should go.

The piano line acts as the hook of the song; it follows the melody closely. At times, acting as a call and response. The guide vocal on the demo is so good that most of it was kept for the final version. Listening to this is a good insight into the process, and both elements can be heard quite effectively on the finished version.

Producer Jim Scott adds some sleigh bells into the mix. It is another one to which Lisa Germano contributes. Her contributions are always welcomed by Neil Finn, as noted when talking about this and her performance on 'Archer's Arrow':

> We finished off some tracks in LA at Jim Scott's studio and Lisa Germano came out for a day and played some beautiful things, as she always does, on 'Even If' and 'Archer's Arrows'. It's always lovely to have her presence.[10]

This is a tender and easy-going song that works well in the running order as a contrast to the preceding songs.

'Elephants'

Written by Neil Finn
Duration: 4:30

A beautiful piano piece that sees out the album. The lyrical content has a good message to ring out on the final track of the album. The arrangement is understated, but if you dig deep, there is a lot to be found in the mix. The percussion is delicate. The piano and the vocals are the dominant components throughout. There are fragments of slide guitar added to the mix that add to the atmospheric nature to the tune. Jim Scott adds elephant footsteps to the mix.

Original Album Extra Tracks

Some editions of the 2010 album come with an instrumental version of 'The Intriguer'.

2016 Deluxe Edition bonus disc (Universal)

This includes the usual number of alternate versions, tracks that did not make the album, and live versions.

Tracklist

'The Only Way to Go Is Forwards' (live), 'Beautiful Life' (live), 'Either Side Of The World' (live), 'Twice If You're Lucky' (live), 'Bound To Rescue' (live), 'God Lives Over The Road' (studio demo), 'Isolation' (studio demo), 'Better Things' (studio demo), 'Even If' (take 1), 'Archers Arrows' (alternative version), 'Saturday Sun' (alternative version), 'The Intriguer', 'Turn It Around', 'Eyes Grow Heavy', 'Two Minutes Of Silence', 'Nonsense Of Course'.

'The Only Way to Go Is Forwards'(live)

Written by Neil Finn
Duration: 5:13

It is another song that the band road-tested live, but despite this, it did not make the running order for the album. It is a very catchy number, but one that did not come together when they were arranging the song for recording. It is a guitar-driven number and sounds like it has great potential. It is songs like this that make deluxe editions like this a must.

In this instance, the *Intriguer* box set, there is almost an album of other tracks that could have made a strong album in their own right. Its omission has left the diehards who will have heard this one performed live wondering how it was not released.

These are the dilemmas that a songwriter of Neil Finn's calibre, who has so many great songs to choose from for each album: 'Somebody referred to that to me and said it's their favourite Crowded House song since the second record. Somebody's always championing something that didn't get a shot. It's nice, really.'[11]

'Beautiful Life' (live)

Written by Neil Finn
Duration: 5:14

From a set of songs played live at Leigh Sawmill Café, New Zealand, in February 2008, this was another not to make the final reckoning for the album. There is a prominent haunting melodica from Mark Hart throughout the song. It is a song with another laid-back, winding melody. It seems fully formed with this version. The studio demo was broadcast on Neil Finn's *Fangradio* show.

'Bound To Rescue' (live)

Written by Neil Finn
Duration: 2:47

For the second deluxe edition running a version of 'Bound to Rescue' has been included as a bonus disc track. This time, it is the live Leigh Sawmills version of the song that misses out on the main album.

On *Time on Earth*, the home demo version was one of the additional tracks. It is unlucky not to have made it onto the *Intriguer* album. It starts off sounding like a Bacharach and David number. It is a heartfelt and tender ballad. Maybe it occupies a similar sonic space as 'Even If' to have been included on *Intriguer.*

It is still a great song and deserving of its space on the deluxe edition.

'God Lives Over the Road' (studio demo)

Written by Neil Finn
Duration: 3:41

This is a largely instrumental track that fans of Neil Finn would have heard previously. It was debuted on the bFM radio series, Neil Finn's *Cornucopia of Flowers*, which has since been replayed on Neil's *Fangradio* show. The inspirations for the title came from close to Neil Finn's studio.

> This was a piece of piano music which I'd written and had for a long time, and we tried to make it into something. The Orange Ballroom was, at the time, next to the Roundhead Studios and across the road, and there was a new Christian gathering in there every couple of days. It was occupied by a young Christian group playing rock music, so that's what the title refers to.[12]

It is a haunting number, where the slide guitar is given prominence. The minimal lyrics are derived from a prayer or sermon and link well with the title.

'Better Things' (studio demo)

Written by Neil Finn
Duration: 3:26

Elements of this sound like the song is fully formed; the mumbled lyrics in parts suggest that this was one that they'd get back to and finish. Another one with potential but never found its way to being released on the album.

It is quite a funky number. There's a great walking bassline from Nick Seymour that moves the song along. The keyboards lock in with the bass to give the song its groove. The shuffle rhythm is used to good effect. The slide guitar gives it an otherworldly quality. The middle 8 has great potential.

'The Intriguer'

Written by Neil Finn
Duration: 3:26

A song in 7/4 time, and again, it is a song title that lent its name to an album but never appeared on the final track list. That's not the case if you had the vinyl version of *Intriguer*—an instrumental of this song can be heard there.

It links to a cartoon by Michael Leunig that depicts the song and appeared in the June 2010 Intriguer Tour programme, The Intriguer being a character that Michael Leunig and Neil Finn invented. The song was originally known as '789'. It has a bouncy, vibrant beat, helped by the busy time signature. The piano-led intro sounds like it is about to break out into the Sesame Street theme song. Likewise, there is the feeling that could make a perfect soundtrack to a cartoon or superhero movie.

The song is a fan favourite live, and the song even had a second life when a different version was written and performed by a fan. When the album was released, an instrumental mix was made available on the band's website for The Intriguer Lyrics Competition. Sarah McCallum's lyrics and vocal melody won the contest. As Miss Little, she joined Crowded House on stage at Sydney's Hordern Pavilion on 6 November 2010 to perform her winning entry.

'Turn It Around'

Written by Neil Finn
Duration: 4:04

It was originally released as an extra track on digital versions of the album. Again, it had been road-tested live before it was recorded for consideration for the album. There is a great piano keyboard line running through this one. The vocal harmonies are excellent throughout. There is a wonderful prog-rock keyboard line on the outro. This has an added euphonium solo to great effect.

Neil Finn was a fan of this too:

> 'Don McGlashan guested on a few songs and played horn. The one song he had a good run on, didn't make the record. People would know that one from the gigs. It turned out well. Maybe it suffered from being one of the first songs that was out there. It didn't measure up in the end. Maybe we never nailed it as well, as it was live either. He plays a ripping euphonium solo in that one.[13]

You can see why Crowded House fans are unsure why this never made it to the physical copy. If volume 2 of *Afterglow* is ever released, this would certainly have to be included. For now, it can be found online and as part of the deluxe editions series.

'Eyes Grow Heavy'

Written by Neil Finn
Duration: 3:42

Another one that was originally released as an extra track on the digital versions of the album. There is a tender vocal arrangement from Finn. This was originally a laid-back piano track, before the choir arrives at the end, providing an effective coda. It is a quietly understated number.

'Two Minutes of Silence'

Written by Neil Finn, Mark Hart, Nick Seymour and Matt Sherrod
Duration: 4:12

A song that was inspired by observing a two-minute silence following the Christchurch earthquake in February 2011.

Nick Seymour discussed the moment and how the song came about.

> I had never been in a situation like that. When we were in the recording studio, ordinarily we would be isolated in this kind of life support bubble—it's like being in outer space when you're in a recording studio—and it was suggested that we observe the two minutes of silence that the whole of New Zealand was observing in memoriam. The song was performed just after we had done that.[14]

The song has a melancholic quality to it. The prominent instrument is a piano/keyboard refrain. It has a hauntingly minimalist arrangement.

Lyrically, it could be seen to reflect the events of the earthquake, but it also had inspirational elements from another historical source, as Neil Finn relates:

> This song arose out of a period of jamming in 2011 with Nick Launay, and it has a lot of atmosphere. I finished 'Two Minutes of Silence' with a view towards it being used for a drama series about Anzac Day in 2015. It didn't end up happening, but its final lyrics are very much in honour of that historical event.[15]

'Nonsense Of Course'

Written by Neil Finn, Mark Hart, Nick Seymour and Matt Sherrod
Duration: 9:05

The track runs to just over nine minutes in length, although there is an Easter egg that's worth sticking around for just after the four-minute mark. This may have been formulated with the band jamming, given the four-way writing credits. It is another insight into the creative process, although these elements may not have been in the running for the album.

There's an impassioned vocal from Neil Finn towards the end of the first part, which caused alarm when Neil Finn performed a version of this one: 'I frightened Nick Launay's neighbour as I sang the end vocal for this at Nick's house in L.A. He came up to see what was happening, to make sure I was OK.'[16]

'Strangest Friends'

Written by Neil Finn

The second part of this sounds to be the more developed of the two ideas included here, but not surprisingly, as fans of Neil Finn could attest to, having already heard a version of this song on his 2014 solo album *Dizzy Heights*. The version that appears here is fuller and has a longer run time than the one eventually released. The chorus will be recognisable to those who have heard the updated version. The recording of the solo version included Sharon and Elroy, making it a real family affair.

To Neil Finn, this is a meditation on the nature of being in a band:

> The relationship between the audience and the performer is an interesting one, and they are like the strangest friends you've got. From both sides. There's a heartfelt sharing of music with people, but you don't get to know them that well, and they don't get to know you that well.[17]

10

The Very, Very Best of Crowded House (2010)

Released in October 2010
Capitol/EMI compilation, sold in various editions (some available in selected territories only) with different covers covering the four seasons:

Autumn:	CD (2-LP edition released globally in 2019)
Winter:	CD and DVD
Spring:	2CD and DVD
Summer:	2CD
Duration:	70:55
Chart positions:	Australia: 11; New Zealand: 12; UK: 49

There is no doubt that the selection of songs could be deemed to be Crowded House at their very best. The addition of the extra very in the title is probably the record label trying to justify the release of another greatest hits collection.

Having released the *Intriguer* album in June 2010, another compilation followed in October of the same year. The band had left Capitol/EMI Records in 2010. It feels like a cynical record label release, cashing in on the band. It lacks the typical Nick Seymour cover design, which is telling, as it shows how involved the band was in the release. Instead, the front cover features a pastiche of past Nick Seymour designs.

The Very, Very Best of Crowded House features nineteen singles from the period covering Crowded House's first five studio albums. Multiple CDs and DVD box sets were made available, which included a DVD of twenty-five of the band's music videos. The album is also available as a 'Deluxe Digital Version', which featured thirty-two tracks including a rare live recording of the band's favourite cover version of the Hunters & Collectors song 'Throw Your Arms Around Me'. Tellingly, there are no extra tracks or missing tracks for diehard fans.

The album is very much in keeping with the 1996 *Recurring Dream* compilation album released at the time of the band's split. Two songs have been added from the 2007 comeback album *Time on Earth*, 'Don't Stop Now' and 'Pour Le Monde'.

Also included are two songs from *Together Alone* ('Fingers of Love' and 'Nails in My Feet') and 'Chocolate Cake' from *Woodface*, which were omitted from the previous compilation. Four early Crowded House singles—'World Where You Live', 'When You Come', 'Into Temptation' and 'I Feel Possessed', which featured on *Recurring Dream*—have not been included on this new album. 'Everything Is Good for You', one of three tracks specially recorded for the 1996 compilation, was also not included.

Disc 1 (CD)

'Something So Strong', 'Weather with You', 'Chocolate Cake', 'Fall at Your Feet', 'Distant Sun', 'Better Be Home Soon', 'Four Seasons in One Day', 'Don't Dream It's Over', 'Mean to Me', 'Locked Out', 'Don't Stop Now', Pineapple Head', 'Instinct', 'Fingers of Love', 'Private Universe', 'Not the Girl You Think You Are', 'Nails in My Feet', 'Pour le Monde'.

CD & DVD box set: Disc 2 (DVD)

'Mean to Me', 'Now We're Getting Somewhere', 'Don't Dream It's Over', 'World Where You Live', 'Something So Strong', Better Be Home Soon', 'When You Come', 'Into Temptation', 'Sister Madly', 'I Feel Possessed', Chocolate Cake', 'Fall at Your Feet', 'It's Only Natural', 'Weather with You', 'Four Seasons in One Day', 'Distant Sun', 'Nails in My Feet', 'Locked Out', 'Private Universe', 'Everything Is Good for You', 'Not the Girl You Think You Are', 'Instinct', 'Don't Stop Now', 'She Called Up', 'Better Be Home Soon'

Deluxe Double-disc version

Disc 1

'Now We're Getting Somewhere', 'World Where You Live', 'Weather with You', 'Something So Strong', 'When You Come', 'Fingers of Love', 'Four Seasons in One Day', 'Distant Sun', 'Don't Stop Now', 'Sister Madly', 'Chocolate Cake', 'Locked Out', 'Never Be the Same', 'Hole in the River', 'Not the Girl You Think You Are', 'Better Be Home Soon'

Disc 2

'Mean to Me', 'It's Only Natural', 'Fall at Your Feet', 'Recurring Dream', Private Universe', 'Pineapple Head', 'She Called Up', 'I Feel Possessed', 'Instinct', 'Everything Is Good for You', 'Into Temptation', 'Nails in My Feet', 'Don't Dream It's Over', 'Pour le Monde', 'Whispers and Moans', 'Throw Your Arms Around Me' (live from the Roxy, Los Angeles, 26 February 1987)

11

Dreamers Are Waiting (2021)

Original Album release:	June 2021 (EMI/Universal)
Personnel:	Neil Finn: vocals, guitars, piano, keyboards and percussion Liam Finn: guitar, vocals and drums Elroy Finn: drums, vocals, guitar and keyboards Nick Seymour: bass, vocals and keyboards Mitchell Froom: keyboards
Recorded by:	David Boucher and Crowded House at Valentine Recording Studios and United Recording Studios, Los Angeles. Additional recording at home in lockdown from Ireland to LA
Duration:	41:53
Produced by:	Crowded House
Chart positions:	Australia: 2; New Zealand: 2; UK: 6

It was another lengthy gap between albums before the first Crowded House album in over eleven years was released. During this period, Neil Finn had released numerous interesting solo projects, keeping him busy. He even found the time to enjoy a stint as a touring member of Fleetwood Mac. It was this experience that made him want to be in a band again. Having concluded his work with Fleetwood Mac, Neil Finn announced in his online journal in December 2019 that Crowded House was in the studio working on a new album.

The band was not now as all-encompassing as it had been for Neil during the 1980s, but it remained a big part of his musical life. After his Fleetwood Mac experience, Neil decided that some changes were in order. Neil asked himself a simple question: how could he reimagine Crowded House so that it would continue to excite him? The answer was closer than he realised. [1]

There would be a shuffling of the deck once again, a time to start developing Crowded House Mark III. Matt Sharrod and Mark Hart were no longer part of the band for this album; they had played their last dates in 2016. This was a line-up that had never quite gelled in Finn's eyes, so it made sense to shake things up with the band.

Neil Finn and Nick Seymour were joined by 'new' recruits, if that is the correct term, Elroy and Liam Finn, who had both appeared as guest musicians on previous Crowded House albums.

Elroy and Liam had both had successful solo careers in their own right before they joined Crowded House. Liam said of the seamlessness of joining the band: 'Both me and Elroy, learnt how to play drums by playing "Fall at Your Feet" without anyone looking at us like it was slow. That was a memorable thing growing up. I think that's why we can slip into this.'[2]

The call to join could have come sooner. Neil Finn reflected on why Elroy was the right choice to join the band as a drummer: 'When we first decided to come back in 2006, we tried out about thirty great drummers, but none of them could play the brushes in the manner Paul [Hester] could. Elroy, who was still at school at the time, could.'[3]

Neil presented his sons with the idea of joining the band. They'd served a kind of apprenticeship playing together as a family and recording and touring with their father under various guises. 'I didn't know what anyone would think. It was just an idea in my brain [but] it seemed so right.'[4]

The band's 'new' keyboard player was Mitchell Froom and the producer of old was also made a full member of the band. He had been instrumental in shaping the sound of the earlier albums, as well as contributing some of the distinctive keyboard parts to many songs. He had been asked to join previously, but had not felt the time was right.

The return of Crowded House looked promising, but that was until they had a global pandemic to contend with. They had a few months before lockdown to record as much as they could before the band fled back to their different parts of the world.

As the world tried to understand the scope and impact of the pandemic, Neil and the others worked from home, sending files to each other via Dropbox. They fine-tuned the songs that they had, and they added a few others along the way. In this way, the album was self-produced. Initially, the album was recorded by David Boucher and Crowded House at Valentine Recording Studios and United Recording Studios, Los Angeles; additional recording took place at various homes during lockdown. The Finns were in LA for the early part of the pandemic.

It is not a 'lockdown album' in the sense that it references the Covid pandemic, but it does evoke the time that it was released. The geographically diverse nature of the band did not deter them from getting the album completed or losing touch with their fan base. There were many online lockdown sessions to keep people entertained. The *Fangradio* platform also more than came into its own in this period.

Dreamers Are Waiting was released on 4 June 2021. There have been no deluxe editions of the album released as yet. The critical response to the album was warm and receptive from most critics.

The artwork was again produced by Nick Seymour, with one of the images described as 'Madonna Overlooking Cityscape with Escaped Bird'.

The album came with a dedication, 'In loving memory of Bones'. The Bones in question was Bones Hillman, the Midnight Oil Bass player of twenty years or so, who died of cancer in November 2020. He was once in the running for the band's bass player, but ultimately lost out to Nick Seymour.

The tracks

'Bad Times Good'

Written by Neil Finn, Liam Finn, Nick Seymour and Elroy Finn
Duration: 3:42

This is a dreamy, ethereal opener. For fans of the band would have been scrutinising this on release to see how the line-up changes would affect the band's sound, they would have been content with the opening number.

The first track is a Crowded House number that appears to have been informed by the evolution of Finn's songwriting throughout his solo career and his work with other musicians, in particular Fleetwood Mac.

The structure is different; it is not the usual verse, big chorus dynamic that you would associate with the band. The chorus introduces the musical motif that runs throughout the song. The number of co-writes indicates that this was one of the songs that might have been put together during lockdown. The files would have been shared via Dropbox, and the song would have developed with the individual members working in isolation. What was achieved is certainly greater than the sum of their parts.

Given what was going on in the world when this was written/recorded, you could read a lot into the lyrics. As ever, the harmonies are to the fore, which gives the song that dreamlike state. The guitar acts as a great hook throughout. The delicate, almost distant piano tinkling away in the background adds to the calm. There is something otherworldly about the song.

While elsewhere on the album we get taken to the island, this song feels like we are there and enjoying the scenery. It is a very reflective opener.

'Playing With Fire'

Written by Neil Finn, Liam Finn, Elroy Finn, Nick Seymour and Mitchell Froom
Duration: 3:28
Released as a single in May 2021

After the relaxed opening number, 'Playing with Fire' sounds recognisably how casual listeners would expect the band to sound on a release in 2021. It is another one of those Crowded House singles that sneaks up on you. The tippy tap percussion is quite infectious. The guitar riff at the start gives way to the rest of the instrumentation as the song ramps up.

All the tricks are used to extenuate the poppy nature of the number. The use of the brass section works well, which Finn has done to similar effect on previous releases. The 'ba-ba-ba' harmonies mirror the brass impeccably, and this helps drive the melody. The extended coda has a dreamy runout that segues nicely into the next song. It sounds as though it were about to evolve into a Pink Floyd number.

The lyrics were written in Los Angeles during lockdown in 2020, and there are oblique references to what the world went through at the time. The upbeat nature of the song belies that time when there was so much uncertainty.

There is a video that shows the newly reconfigured band back in the room after the lockdowns. They seem to be having a great time filming this. This is the third single to be released from the album, and it was released in May 2021.

It is another co-write, this time with all members contributing.

'To The Island'

Written by Neil Finn
Duration: 3:59
Released as a single in February 2021

The previous number slowly evolves into the next track. It is another song that was released during lockdown. The song always evokes that time whenever I hear it. I do not know whether it's just the title or the lyrical references to being 'in our little worlds'.

The vocal hook at the start works well. So too does Finn's call-and-response, almost arguing with himself. The harmonies are brilliant too. The chorus is as hooky as ever. The instrumentation is quite minimalist. There is a very Beatlesque middle eight. The extended guitar jam at the end sounds like musicians who have been frustrated by being in lockdown, finally being able to let loose in a studio again.

The track leaves enough there that it is open to be reinterpreted. There are a couple of distinctive remixes of the songs that were released on vinyl. The first one, the Tame Impala mix, certainly does not hold back with the deconstruction of the song. There is minimal instrumentation with Finn's vocals. These elements then mutate into heavily treated forms with sounds that come from an exotic island background. It sounds like what you would expect a Tame Impala interpretation of a Crowded House song should sound like.

Neil Finn was impressed by what became of this song:

> With all the world upended and nothing in its right place, we became curious to hear how our favourite contemporary musicians and record makers might reimagine a Crowded House song. I emailed our version of 'To The Island' to Kevin Parker (Tame Impala) with an invitation to take it apart and reassemble

> in his own unique way. Happily, he really liked the song and it was an absolute delight to hear what he made from it, an exotic fantasy, I would call it.[5]

The second remix came from The Unknown Mortal Orchestra, who reinterpreted the song more dynamically. The backing is more industrial.

Again, Neil Finn loved the way the song had been reinterpreted:

> Another artist we in Crowded House greatly admire is fellow New Zealander Ruban Neilson [of Unknown Mortal Orchestra]. Ruban was willing and able when asked to dismantle our single 'To The Island'. His remix has reimagined our song with swagger and grit and some glam overtones... we think it's transformed in a beautiful way.[6]

The original song came out in February 2021 in digital formats. The two remixes were released in April 2021 and are available on individual 7-inch vinyl editions, as well as to download and stream.

The official video was directed by Neil Finn and Simon Mark Brown and does a good job of constructing a narrative of the band arriving on the island to play.[7] The Finns seem to be all present and correct following their journeys to get to the venue. Neil Finn seemingly had to navigate his journey by boat at one stage. Mitchell Froom had the best journey of them all, via limousine. Nick Seymour and Mitchell Froom are superimposed reasonably well to give the impression that they were all together in the room.

The process of putting something together like this was made all the more difficult given that global travel was still an issue when the video was being filmed. They have done a good job putting something together that has an effective narrative.

'Sweet Tooth'

Written by Neil Finn
Duration: 3:13
Released as a single January 2022

It opens with a bit of scratchy guitar and a bluesy keyboard riff. There is some slide guitar in the mix, too. This adds to the off-kilter nature of what the song is trying to represent.

There is a great Nick Seymour bass line that underpins this song. The keyboard line has an endearing hook to it. There is a charming sing-along chorus, as ever. It is another one of those songs that seems to be bobbing along nicely before it twists and turns. The middle eight has a giddiness that feels like a sugar rush in musical form. There is a great guitar solo over the breakdown.

Despite the perkiness of the arrangement, there is a melancholic edge to the song. As the world looked back to a far-off, better time, Finn wanted the video to capture a childhood memory that the song evokes: 'I wanted to have pictures that represented the giddy euphoria of eating sweets when you are a kid, a kind of sensory overload that resembles a drug experience.'[8]

The video is a straightforward band-in-a-room format, albeit a luxury in that era. The video is treated with effects to give it the experience that Finn wanted to reflect.[9]

'Whatever You Want'

Written by Neil Finn
Duration: 3:22
Released as a single October 2020

This is a song that possibly owes its presence on the album to Neil's grandson, Buddy. He was heard singing it around the house when it was being written. This one-person focus group saw the song taken apart and put back together many times before the band got it right.

It was recorded live in one room, after which everyone disappeared into little bunkers to work on their parts.

It opens with another exceptional Nick Seymour bassline, and this hook continues throughout the song. There is a great groove to the song, supplied by Elroy Finn. From a production point of view, a lot of work went into getting the sound right. Mitchell Froom delivers a growly, distorted keyboard to add to the mix.

The arpeggiated guitar part locks in excellently with the bassline. The harmonies and lead vocals are very catchy. The outro ramps up the instrumentation to eleven.

The track arrives with a video, directed by Nina Ljeti and starring musician Mac DeMarco. The band do not appear in the video, given that it was released during Covid. It is quite a quirky take on the song.[10]

In a time of Donald Trump, it is hard not to think these impassioned lines are about him. Finn said on his *Fangradio* show that the song was inspired by the yes-men and the enablers in the world. Sometimes, they are the voices in your head. Neil Finn has also said that the song is more of a hangover song, waking up with fear after last night's revelry. We can all relate to that.[11]

This is the band's first single to be released in ten years. It might not be a single that will get new fans on board, but there is enough here for the diehards to love.

'Show Me the Way'

Written by Neil Finn
Duration: 3:44

There are numerous ways to listen to a Crowded House album these days. As the vinyl revival was in full swing at this point, for those who have the vinyl edition, this is the perfect conclusion to side one. The chiming guitars in the intro evoke something reminiscent of Pink Floyd's 'Wish You Were Here'.

This is a more introspective number for the middle of the record (or end of side one if that is your preferred style of listening). This song adopts a style akin to the latter solo releases from Neil Finn. There is a beautiful vocal melody running throughout this one. The tender guitar sound, paired with the fragile vocals, works well. The bass sounds like it might be played on an upright bass, as opposed to the standard rock form. Nick Seymour is suited to this style of playing.

Some editions of the album incorrectly credit this to Liam Finn, but this is a Neil Finn composition. [12]

'Goodnight Everyone'

Written by Liam Finn
Duration: 3:31

Liam gets his first solo songwriting credit on the album. He also gets to sing this one. The vocal stylings of Neil and Liam sound interchangeable, so you could miss that the vocal duties have been shared at this point.

It has an atmospheric ambience. The shimmering, echoey guitars throughout give it an ethereal quality. There is an understated bassline that drives this along. These elements, in combination with the delicately strummed guitar, give this a countrified feel. The dreamy vocals also give the song a spectral charm. Is it a meditation on fame, or is it a lullaby? Whatever it is, it is one of the hidden gems on the album.

Given the issues with lockdown, there are not many guest musicians on the record; this is one of the few numbers that has extras. For instance, Eliza-Jane Barnes provides backing vocals. The daughter of Australian singer Jimmy Barnes, she is someone who Liam Finn had previously worked with.

'Too Good for This World'

Written by Neil Finn and Tim Finn
Duration: 3:40

A Finn Brothers collaboration that is acoustic and sounds like a throwback to a different age. The plucked guitar sounds like it is performed on an old-style lap steel guitar

The brushes for percussion are used quite successfully. Elroy was taught all he knew in terms of playing in this style by Paul Hester. Listening to this, it feels like a passing of the flame from one drummer to the other. Crowded House have always incorporated this style effectively, whether on a record or in their stripped-back shows earlier in their career.

It sounds laid-back and sparse, but that is part of its charm. The band seem to be all there, but the vocals and the guitar are upfront in the mix. The song was earmarked for another collection of songs, as Neil Finn recounted:

> It was originally written for a musical that Tim and I were working on that didn't get off the ground. Like other songs, including 'Won't Give In' and 'To the Island'... songs that got left on the cutting room floor.[13]

The musical in question was to be based on Mervyn Peake's 1953 novel *Mr Pye*, which is '...about a guy who is consumed by the evangelical urge to go to the island of Sark and shower it with kindness and love to turn it into a sort of heaven on earth'.[14]

Where the song ended up is quite fitting given its inspiration.

'Start Of Something'

Written by Liam Finn and Neil Finn
Duration: 3:20

Neil and Liam Finn had previously collaborated on their 2018 album *Lightsleeper*. Inevitably, that pairing has teamed up again under the guise of Crowded House. It is a song that would have fitted seamlessly into that collaboration.

Amazing harmonies and outstanding melodies are at the forefront of this one. It is both cinematic in its scope, while also being intimate. There are delicate guitar lines which ring throughout. This gives the song a campfire or torchlight feel. The guitar at the outro locks in well with the melody.

Lyrically, there is a lot to read into this. Maybe a lockdown-inspired song, or it could be about the end or start of a relationship. It is another of the understated highlights of the album.

'Real Life Woman'

Written by Neil Finn
Duration: 3:48
Released as a single

The descending chord pattern and the relaxed rhythm track sound very Beatlesque. The vocal harmonies, as ever, are pinpoint. The lyrical refrain of 'a real-life woman' is very catchy. The lead vocals and the harmonies are very captivating, too. The middle eight ramps up the Beatleisms even more. The song builds quite effectively in the instrumental part with what feels like a dramatic ending. This fits well with the noirish nature of the lyrics. It might sound like a typical Crowded House song, but the way that it unfolds offers up something different for the listener.

Lyrically, the first line may throw the listener off as to what the song is about, especially with the 'No I'll never understand, the criminal mind' lines. The imagery that the song portrays is very film noir; it might be Neil Finn reflecting on a late-night detective movie that he has just seen.

'Love Isn't Hard At All'

Written by Elroy Finn and Neil Finn
Duration: 3:02

Having written with Liam, Neil collaborates with his other son, Elroy. The song was not technically released as a single, but a video was produced to accompany the song.

The video was produced by Neil Finn, using footage from surfing legend Kelly Slater. The band has also collaborated on designs for the sustainable clothing brand, Outerknown, co-founded by Kelly Slater. Talking about the collaboration on the band's website, Neil Finn said:

> 'Love Isn't Hard At All' and doesn't Kelly Slater make it look easy? The sentiments and energy of our song seemed perfectly in synch with the flow and focus of the surfing world's most gifted expressionist. World Surf League and Kelly supplied footage of some of his recent incredible waves, which I was delighted to edit together for this visual tribute to his power and grace.[15]

The song was written mainly by Elroy. It included elements from the theme music from Tetris, which is derived from the Russian folk song 'Korobeiniki'. This is an upbeat and energetic number. Elroy gets to highlight his talent on the drums (and as a songwriter) to good effect. After a run of relaxed and chilled-out songs, this is an arresting diversion from that calm. Sharon Finn makes it a family affair with backing vocals.

'Deeper Down'

Written by Neil Finn
Duration: 3:13
Released as a single

A percussive sound and a shuffle beat announce the last number on the album. It is another peaceful and reflective number. The upbeat nature of the arrangement belies the lyrics. The extended instrumental section has a contemplative feel to it. Neil Finn employs his falsetto vocal style to good effect, as if the song were being whispered in your ear.

It a song that fits well as the last track of this album: though a bit too fragile to be employed live, it is a great song all the same.

12

Gravity Stairs (2024)

Album release:	May 2024 (BMG) CD, Vinyl, Blu-Ray ATMOS
Personnel:	Neil Finn: vocals, guitars, piano, keyboards and bass Nick Seymour: bass, vocals and keyboards Liam Finn: guitar and vocals Elroy Finn: drums, guitar, vocals and keyboards Mitchell Froom: keyboards Steven Schram: production, mixing and electric guitar on 'The Howl' and 'I Can't Keep Up with You' Bob Ludwig: engineering Paul Taylor: percussion Sharon Finn: additional vocals on 'Magic Piano' and 'All That I Can Ever Own' Ladyhawke: additional vocals on 'Teenage Summer' Tim Finn: additional vocals on 'Some Greater Plan (for Claire)' Antonis Moriatis: bouzouki on 'Some Greater Plan (for Claire)' Elias Dendias: bouzouki on 'Some Greater Plan (for Claire) Nassos Vlachos: guitar on 'Some Greater Plan (for Claire)' Tryfon Baitsis: guitar on 'Some Greater Plan (for Claire)' Lauryn Canny: additional backing vocals on 'Black Water, White Circle' and additional vocals on 'Blurry Grass' and 'Thirsty' Eliza-Jane Barnes: additional vocals on 'Thirsty'

	Jimmy Metherell: additional vocals on 'Thirsty'
	Zoe Moon: additional vocals on 'Night Song'
Duration:	40:40
Recorded and mixed by:	Steven Schram
Produced by:	Crowded House & Steven Schram
Charts:	Australian: 3; New Zealand: 4; UK: 8

There was a more conventional approach to the writing and recording of the eighth studio album. It was also a quicker turnaround between albums this time around. The line-up had stayed intact between albums, and their experiences for the last album had revitalised Neil Finn and his band.

There were no restrictions that affected the line-up like during the run-up and release of *Dreamers Are Waiting*. When the restrictions enforced because of COVID were lifted, the band spent a great deal on the road, increasing the band's cohesion as a result. This was something that carried through to the new album.

This is something that Neil Finn has noted: 'I think the result of quite a bit of touring has made the band more solid, more expressive and more creative and more willing to take risks. The trust level has gone up.'[1]

Making a Crowded House album is more complicated these days, given that its members are scattered across four different countries: Neil Finn in New Zealand, Nick Seymour in Ireland, Mitchell Froom and Liam Finn in Los Angeles and Elroy Finn in London. As Neil Finn explained to *Classic Pop* in 2024, 'We're trying to be as far away from each other as possible, and we're doing it very well.'[2]

The geographical issues are not a problem for the band, and the opportunities to play together are a lot easier than they were for the previous record. Despite this, they still deployed several of the methods used for the making of *Gravity Stairs*:

> We are spread out about as far as you could be, but we had a good amount of practice with international record-making over the Covid period [with Dreamers Are Waiting], so it's not something that's too foreign. There's been a lot of file sharing involved, but I think the results are unique and cool for that reason, too.[3]

The initial sessions for *Gravity Stairs* began almost by accident when the band were together while rehearsing for an upcoming tour. Those sessions in Byron Bay in 2022 saw the line-up trying out a couple of the new songs and recording them.

Liam Finn reflected on the success of those early sessions:

> The original tracks that we did in Byron Bay were lush and kind of milky sounding, and the majority of the record is from that first couple of weeks. We were supposed to be quarantining before a tour, and we thought we'd

> rehearse three songs but wound up doing about nine. We were learning to play the songs and not expressly thinking that we were making a record, so there's a nice nonchalant looseness to them.[4]

The sessions there saw them connect with local producer Steven Schram, who ended up producing and engineering the record. His work was acknowledged when he was nominated (along with the band) for an ARIA (Australian Recording Industry Association) Award in 2024, in the producer category for 'Best Produced Release'.

One of the first songs that came together for the album was 'Magic Piano'. This came about in the old-fashioned, band-on-the-floor (approach), working things out and playing as a whole live band.[5] For Neil Finn, the process of putting together the album and that song was about trying to make a sound that is the total of their personalities.[6]

Crowded House is one of many strands for Neil Finn these days, and often the solo aspects of his career have merged into his work with the band. It feels like the focus of the writing for the album was mainly focussed on a new Crowded House record. There have been times when Crowded House albums have emerged out of solo projects and vice versa.

Neil Finn explained his songwriting process to *Rock Cellar* in 2024:

> It's really just the creative process of working them up into songs that the band becomes involved with. The process of writing, getting ideas and making little demos at home is the same, no matter whether it's solo or Crowded House or whatever. There might be the odd occasion where a song will come along that doesn't sound like it needs a band to play on it. But that's OK too, because we're a very flexible band. We can create an atmosphere. We don't have to be rocking the pop combo thing the whole time either. It's becoming a lot broader and we're getting into areas that we didn't before, which is what bands should always be doing.[7]

It is very much a band record, something Neil Finn is pleased with: 'You can sit around and subvert the process as a band. When you're solo, sometimes it feels a little bit earnest and a bit lonely. So having a band is fantastic.'[8]

Back on the album and tour cycle, 2024 saw the band tour extensively around the world: US, Europe—including a trip to The Cavern in Liverpool, where they played to less than 400 fans, despite more than 30,000 other fans trying to book tickets[9]—and finally Australia and New Zealand.

It is a very mellow contemplative album. At times, the album has a dreamy quality to it. It veers into more progressive psychedelic musical territories for possibly the first time in their career.

The album was the second by Crowded House Mk III and was well-received by the critics and by their fans, which is reassuring for the band., Anticipating the thrill of playing the new songs live, Neil Finn said: 'You never know whether it's going to connect with people, but we get the sense that it is connecting already, and we know it'll be an amazing record to play.'[10]

When they did get to play, they could sense that the songs were landing with their fans:

> There was not a flood of people heading to the bar. That's always the sign you look for with new songs. I think we're playing them well and they have an integrity onstage that people are recognising. Also, one of the nice things about having a long-term relationship with an audience is not relying on the current hit or single. People come with an open mind expecting to hear deviations and diversions.[11]

Having had numerous comparisons to The Beatles down the years musically, the artwork for the album is a nod to an album from the Fab Four. This again was designed by Nick Seymour, and the hand-drawn cartoons of the band are similar in style to Klaus Voormann's style for the 1966 album, *Revolver* by The Beatles.

The album was released on vinyl, CD, streaming, and download, as well as a Blu-Ray (Dolby Atmos) edition. At the time of print, a deluxe edition has not yet been released.

The tracks

'Magic Piano'

Written by Neil Finn
Duration: 4:47

The song that kickstarted the sessions for *Gravity Stairs* and its one that sets the tone for the record. The dreamy atmosphere of the opener is a sound that permeates the record. It is a perfect start to the album.

The song started out being one of the most complex demos written for the album, which the band deconstructed to form something simpler. The finished track is the sound of the band playing in the room; the vocals were done separately. It has a complex arrangement and evolved during these initial sessions.

The arrangement has a trance-like opening. Nick Seymour's bass is, as ever, lyrical and melodic. It is an excellent counter-balance to all the other elements going on in the song. Mitchell Froom's Hammond organ adds to the dream-like state, so too do the beautiful descending piano motifs. Sharon Finn adds the beautiful female harmonies, which act as a call and response. Liam Finn's guitar is very textured throughout.

It was clear that the band had captured something definitive, and it earned its place as the opening number. As Neil Finn explains: 'We were aware that we had made something with great beauty and integrity. It felt like a definitive statement and that it should be the first track on the record.'[12]

The song contains the album's title in the lyrics. The theme of the song on one level, could appear as being quite abstract, but in effect, it has weighty concerns regarding mortality. It is also a paean to the joys of melody, as in 'let the melody reign, oh yeah'. Musically, it is equally meditative and reflective.

To Neil Finn, the song contemplates the process of songwriting and 'waiting on the promise of a great new magic tune to appear. But be aware that you have to climb these stairs to get to it.'[13]

The gravity stairs are not just about the mortal, but also have a metaphorical inspiration, inspired by an actual stone staircase leading up to the Finns' holiday home in Greece. 'I've lugged bags up there many times.'[14]

The title of the song was inspired by the Magic Piano from a children's radio show from the 1940s. Neil Finn explained how the inspirations of this show led to the song being a reflection on his craft as a songwriter:

> The radio show is about a kid who hates practising piano, and his piano starts to talk to him, and then he becomes able to play incredible things on his piano because the piano is sort of doing it all. And so, some of the themes were sparked by that. But then, it is a genuinely a genuine love song to my piano. It's also got other things to it, about music in general—just the effort to achieve lightness and elevation, and how magical that the whole thing is. I suppose I'm also stating my absolute devotion to melody as the lead—how it takes the lead part in my relationship with music. [15]

There are many great lines throughout the song, but this may be the best: 'If I end up forgetting what I had to say, you will still hear me humming on the last day.' This one line sums up the song, which is a tender reflection on music and getting old.

'Teenage Summer' (previously known as Life's Imitation)

Written by Neil Finn
Duration: 3:42
Released as a single in April 2024

We have already heard from the next generation of Finns, but the title of this one was shaped by Neil's grandson Manaia. 'Teenage Summer' was his favourite song. Neil Finn said about the evolution of the song title: 'He'd identified the peak moment in the song, and a light went on. It is that simple: the children must be heard.'[16]

Buddy, Neil's other grandson, shaped the track 'Whatever You Want' on the previous album. His two grandsons' interventions may have pointed the way for the direction of the band in the future: 'We've got Mach Two—well, probably Mach Three—version of Crowded House to groom now.'[17]

It is listed on the vinyl and the CD as 'Life's Imitation'; on the digital version, it shows its new title. It had several outings under its old title. Neil Finn thought that they had blundered with the initial name of the song: '"Life's Imitation" isn't quite as good a name, really, but initially I thought that was the big hook. "Teenage Summer" was the throwaway at the end, but it's become a rallying cry of sorts.'[18]

It was a song inspired by the time of COVID. 'It's about trying to achieve some reality and being aware that connection is hard to make,' he says. 'And even before COVID, it was hard to find closeness to people. That became particularly acute afterwards.'[19]

It opens with what Liam Finn describes as 'the classic Dad's strum'.[20] It is another song that is chock-full of vocal harmonies and a longing for a far-off, better time. Instead of wallowing in the melancholy of lockdowns, it is an empathetic take on how things could be. The trademark lush Neil Finn vocal is augmented on this track with a fellow New Zealander—Pip Brown (aka Ladyhawke). The coda returns to the hook of the song.

It was described by Zane Lowe as a '...New Zealand version of "Boys of Summer".'[21] He may have said that with a tongue firmly planted in cheek, but he is right: the song evokes summers of old perfectly.

It was the second single to be released in the run-up to the album release. The video has some of the bookish elements that can be seen in the artwork of the album. [22] The mystical and the fantastical animations are mixed with the band playing together live in the room. It may be the hand of Nick Seymour that is painting the picture of the child at the piano at the start. The video is produced, written and directed by Richard Lowenstein, Andrew de Groot and Lynn-Maree Milburn.

'The Howl'

Written by Liam Finn
Duration: 3:27
Released as a single in May 2024

This was initially intended to be on Liam Finn's solo album, *The Hyperverse* (a version can be found on that album). It was a song that Liam presented to his Dad who picked it off a Pro Tools selection that he had been given when Crowded House was midway through the *Gravity Stairs* sessions.[23] The lyrics were written in the shower by Liam, a place where he has said he often finds inspiration.

The singing and writing credits are shared among the Finn family. A passing listener would think this was Neil singing, but it is Liam who's on vocal duties. The song has all the hallmarks of a classic Crowded House song. The harmonies are perfect as ever. There is a distinct guitar line that has a *Together Alone* vibe about it. The rhythm section is set back but it helps to drive the song. Mitchell Froom has added some beautiful, delicate textures throughout. There are even some howls hidden in the mix.

A YouTube explainer by Liam Finn shows how much has gone into the song. Even with all these elements, it still sounds light and airy, not overdone. Another unassuming but effective track on the album.

The third track to be released as a single, and one that came out on the day of the release of the album. The video takes us back to the beach, not Karekare this time, but the equally beautiful Te Henga, West Auckland. [24] The band are not involved in the video, which features Lee Smith-Gibbons as 'The Woman', Greg Smith as 'The Wolfman' and Breeze as 'The Horse'.

The woman can be seen drawing circles in the sand as a man in a wolf costume rides towards her, whom she seemingly decapitates, but then falls in love with. I am not sure that this description is doing it justice; it really needs to be seen first-hand. On some level, it is a literal interpretation of the lyrics of the song. The video was directed by Aidee Walker and produced by Alexander Gandar.

'All That I Can Ever Own'

Written by Neil Finn
Duration: 3:05

Another introspective number in which Neil Finn reflects on the meaning of love:

> There's an awareness that you can't control the outcomes of what happens when you love someone. Throughout your life, there's an element of letting go of anything other than the love you feel for somebody.[25]

It is a contemplative, gently strummed number. The arrangement again is not too overladen. There are occasional guitar textures throughout. The bass is the most prominent element of the instrumentation on the track. Sharon Finn can be heard adding her warm-hearted background vocals. The middle eight ramps up the arrangement with a passionate vocal from Neil Finn. There may be a banjo in the mix, too. It sounds like that is the last note that rings out of the song.

A pleasant tune that fits in with the overall style of the album.

'Oh Hi'

Written by Neil Finn
Duration: 2:59
Released as a single in February 2024

The first single from the album is a hooky sub-three-minute tune with a memorable chorus. It has the potential to be an ever-present singalong song for fans of the band at future gigs. The chorus sounds like it features a choir to sing this. It could be that the wonders of multitracking in the studio have given the song that wall-of-sound style.

A distinctive song deserves an idiosyncratic video, and that is what it got. Looking for something unusual, directors Daniel Fradin and Kyle Rosenbluth came up with the idea of putting Neil Finn's head onto a young boy's body, creating a young Neil Finn who dances and runs around Brooklyn with a childlike freedom.[26] Appearing in the video are Calvin Knegten as a young Neil Finn and Neil Finn as himself.

There was also an additional video in support of a charity close to the band's heart, So They Can, which supports schools in East Africa. The song was inspired by children at Aberdare Ranges School, Kenya who also appear in the video.[27] There is a reference to the charity appeal: 'Be the one in a million that could lift the sun'.

The tune had been around before the time of the band's involvement, but it was updated to fit the appeal, having found a lyrical thread. Created for and inspired by Neil, who wanted the song to stand up on its own without the backstory.[28] The song has extra depth and meaning for Finn now as a result.

In 2024, the song was one of the songs chosen to feature on BBC Radio 2's Piano Room Month Series. The band performed this alongside the BBC Concert Orchestra.

'Some Greater Plan (for Claire)'

Written by Neil Finn and Tim Finn
Duration: 4:11
Released as a single in October 2024

The album has already spanned the generations of the Finn family, from grandson-inspired titles through to this tender song inspired by Neil Finn's father, Richard.

It is a tune that goes a long way back and is another of the ideas that Neil and Tim Finn had written for a musical that never got off the ground.

The idea for the song was inspired by their father's war diary, which captured a memory of a whirlwind romance when he was stationed in Italy with a girl called Nada met in the Baglioni Ballroom, Florence.

As Neil Finn explained to *Stereogum*:

> And he looked across the room, and there was this glamorous girl who has turned out to be a diplomat's daughter.' He says in his diary, 'She was out of my league, but I asked her to dance and she said, "Yes."' And then they started a lovely two-week, three-week romance while he was in Florence. It became part of the family mythology because dad only knew about six phrases of Italian, but he'd bring them out every time we went to a restaurant or something. [Finn affects a slight Italian accent to imitate his dad speaking] '*Arrivaderci!*' or '*Grazi!*' '*Prego!*' And my mother would roll her eyes and go, 'I suppose that's what [she] used to say.' It became a joke in the family. That was the origin of the first verse of the song. And then it became a little bit more universal in its intent as it goes on. But it is a lovely story. That's what you want when you get caught up in the romance of a moment.[29]

The song has a Mediterranean feel to it, which sees the band complemented by Elias Dendias and Antonis Moriatis on bouzouki, and Nasos Vlachos and Tryfon Baitsis on guitar. These elements add a distinct flavour to the song. The musicians have toured with the band a few times and can be seen in the official video. The Finn brothers' distinctive two-part harmonies are used to good effect, too. They have captured the essence of something with the song, and Neil Finn believes that most of the first take remains in the song.

As well as the theme of being about his father, for Finn, writing in his online journal, the song also explores one of the overarching themes of the album:

> It is somewhat of a homage to my dad, Richard Finn, and a wartime romance he wrote about in his diary. In a broader sense, it refers to the idea that each time we gather for music, we conjure up the spirits of those who went before and revitalise our will to express love and look forward. That's the magical gift of music. [30]

For the broadcaster and fellow New Zealander, Zane Lowe thinks that it is '...a beautiful song, and I think also the band has brought it to life in a wonderful way. It feels almost like a distant relation to "Magic Piano."'[31]

Listening to the song on its own is quite emotional, and the video takes that feeling to the next level.[32] This again was a family affair. It was directed by Neil Finn and Marc Swadel. It starts with the dedication in 'Memory of Richard George Finn, NZ 5th Field Reg 1942–45, who passed away in 2019'. The video features Lauryn Canny and Elroy Finn, who depict the couple who met in that ballroom in Florence. Lauryn also happens to be Elroy's girlfriend, giving the scenes that emotional significance. The scenes of the couple enjoying their time together are interspersed with footage of the band playing together in what looks like the place where the Finns have their holiday home.

It is a beautiful way to end the first side of the vinyl record.

'Black Water, White Circle'

Written by Neil Finn
Duration: 3:43

The song is mysterious and dreamy. It is another ethereal number. Neil Finn has talked about the new Crowded House being not just about melodies but also textures. This is one song that highlights all that is good about the band. The ear for melody is evident for all to hear, but the elements that go into this song are worthy of repeat listens.

The opening notes suggest that this might be a more countrified song, but it soon evolves into something more otherworldly. The time signature of the song is not standard. On first listen, it does not sound like a complicated number, but there are a lot of intricacies and textures in the song. Especially from Mitchell

Froom's keyboard parts. The arpeggiated guitar line that runs through this locks in with the keyboard delightfully. Nick Seymour's basslines are set back in the mix; this is less about the low end for once, but their presence fits the song. The vocal harmonies are woven through this song brilliantly. They include backing vocals from Lauryn Canny, who can be seen in the 'Some Greater Plan (for Clare)' video.

Lyrically, the dreamlike state is summoned throughout. It is another contemplative track about the gravity stairs and mortality. It is another of the songs on the album that at first may not be an obvious standout, but repeat listens unlock many of its charms.

'Blurry Grass'

Written by Elroy Finn and Neil Finn
Duration: 3:09

This is another woozy, dreamlike number, with textures and melodies heard on previous songs on the album coming to the fore again. Elroy Finn took the lead on this one, with a little help from his dad.

Talking to Zane Lowe, Neil Finn said about Elroy's contribution to the album:

> He came up with a demo. It had certain bits of atmosphere that I liked. Sometimes, the magic of a demo is hard to recreate. In modern times, it is easier to integrate those little magic things on demos. So, we chased that thing, and then we added to it, we made it bigger, we moved a few things around, but it was very much Elroy's idea.[33]

For Zane Lowe, 'Blurry Grass' has 'a sound that he had not heard before. It finds a new space to exist,' on a Crowded House record. [34]

It opens up in familiar musical territory. The guitars are straightforward, and Nick Seymour provides one of the walking basslines he does so well. The instrumental interlude at the one-minute thirty-second mark is where the song evolves into the new space that Lowe talks about. Elroy and Lauryn Canny team up again to deliver effective vocal harmonies. Lyrically, the song evokes the spectral as much as the haunting tones of the music.

'I Can't Keep Up with You'

Written by Liam Finn and Neil Finn
Duration: 4:01

After several songs that are big on texture and detail, once the intro is taken care of, this settles down into a more straightforward rocker. That said, there are a few twists and turns along the way that are in keeping with the rest of the album.

The choppy guitars are allied with a driving bass line and your standard drum track. It is probably the most conventional song on the album. It has a post-punk new wave feel to it; I could hear elements of Squeeze or XTC in the mix. It could also be a song that could launch a new Split Enz record.

Lyrically, it is hard to pin this one down, but there are some great allusions to Byron and the Marquis de Sade. It might not have the same lyrical depth as some of the other songs, but it is throwaway in an admirable way.

'Thirsty'

Written by Elroy and Neil Finn
Duration: 3:30

Another song that shows how the collaborative process works so effectively, both musically and lyrically, for the latest iteration of Crowded House. Using Elroy's chords and arrangement, Neil Finn found a melody to go with the pre-existing instrumental track.

There has been no evidence of the generational differences in the band showing so far musically; the Finns are seemingly all on the same page as far as the arrangements go. Lyrically, this song might have highlighted a generational difference. The word Thirsty has taken on a different connotation for a younger group, as Neil Finn observed to Stereogum in 2024:

> The first line I got was, 'How come some people never get thirsty?' And it always seemed a little bit like, 'Can I get behind that thought?' even though it's completely true and we know people who never drink water. But I had to find some deeper significance. Elroy helped me out with that by saying that the young kids these days say if you're thirsty, you're wanting to hook up with people. It's a new expression. I was so relieved to hear that, because I had another angle all of a sudden. 'How come some people never get thirsty?' is about the reluctance to get involved with people. That's the lyric that emerged from it. With all of my lyrics, they're a little ambiguous in places. I like to leave doors open for people to have their own imagination. But that's the setting of it, is a reluctance to jump in and get involved, probably because of the fear of experience and things going badly wrong. It was a lovely development from Elroy and me talking about what the intent of the song should be. And a most welcome thing to be working with my son like that.[35]

It is a more conventional song, which is primarily an acoustic number with added touches of atmospheric slide guitar. The vocal harmonies, as ever, are the fore and delivered perfectly.

'Night Song'

Written by Neil Finn
Duration: 4:14

The intro sounds like a typical piano-led song with added atmospherics. Then the song evolves into an unfamiliar arrangement. This is not the usual style for a Crowded House number. It moves between different time signatures quite seamlessly. The typical verse-chorus song structure would be better described as movements. Though there are three distinct parts on the track, there could have been more.

Speaking to *Guitar Player* magazine in August 2024, Neil Finn explained how the song came about:

> The whole thing came from a jam I had on a Prophet synthesiser. I don't know how to play a synthesiser, but I found a sound on it that was really fun. It had overtones and was suggestive of different chords, and I just jammed over it for half an hour and made a twenty-minute piece of music from it by adding guitars and piano before I even tried to make it into a song. And that delivered the closing track on the record. If you use headphones, you'll hear in the background a woozy, curly little synthesiser sound that was the original impetus for the song.[36]

The song initially was not conceived as a band track for Crowded House, but it fits the album perfectly.[37] Neil Finn said that a lot more of the song exists, and it might appear at some point in the future: 'There are another six parts to that jam, which may emerge. They may begin the next record, who knows? It was a fertile half hour spent learning to play a new instrument.'[38]

It was a song that Neil Finn had long before the band got together for the sessions for the album. Elroy played drums on an early version. The vocals from Neil Finn and Zoe Moon are equally matched, and they balance out really well in the final mix.

Neil Finn explains the inspirations for the song:

> People will certainly relate to the idea that no matter what you're thinking about at two in the morning, it feels like an obsession. And when I'm working on songs, that's the reality: I'm going to bed with a tune going round in my head, and I'll wake up with a tune going round in my head.[39]

As for the unknown man's voice sampled at the end of the song, he says:

> That was inspired by a guy I heard outside my hotel window at three in the morning. He was ranting and saying amazing things. You share that part of the night with people who are on his kind of trip. I felt a strange kinship with him.[40]

That came from the same source as the muse for the song.

13

Neil Finn: The Solo Years (1995–2025)

1. The Finn Brothers—*Finn* (1995)
2. Neil Finn—*Try Whistling This* (1998)
3. Neil Finn—*One Nil* (2001)
4. Various—*Rain* (Soundtrack) (2001)
5. Various—*7 Worlds Collide(Live at The St. James)* (2001)
6. *One All* (2022)
7. The Finn Brothers—*Everyone is Here* (2004)
8. Various—*7 Worlds Collide—Sun Came Out* (2009)
9. Pajama Club—*Pajama Club* (2011)
10. Neil Finn And Paul Kelly—*Goin' Your Way (Live)* (2013)
11. Neil Finn—*Dizzy Heights*(2014)
12. Neil Finn—*Out of Silence* (2017)
13. Neil Finn and Liam Finn *Lightsleeper* (2018)
14. Neil Finn—*Solo at The Seymour Centre, 2010* (2020)
15. Neil Finn—*Sessions at West 54th(Live)* (2025)

I. The Finn Brothers—*Finn* (1995)

Original album release on CD:	November 1995 (Parlophone/Discovery)
Two-disc vinyl edition release:	July 2022 (Needle Mythology)
Two-disc CD edition release:	November 2023 (Needle Mythology)
Personnel:	Tim Finn: vocals, acoustic rhythm guitar, keyboards and drums Neil Finn: vocals, electric rhythm and lead guitar and bass guitar

	Dave Dobbyn: bass guitar on 'Kiss the Road of Rarotonga'
Duration:	38:26
Recorded and mixed at:	York Street Studios, Auckland, November 1994–March 1995
Produced by:	Tchad Blake, Neil Finn and Tim Finn

The first Finn Brothers' album, *Finn*, released in 1995, was a long time coming. The initial sessions for a collaborative album started in 1986. In the six years it took to release *Finn*, a lot had happened. The story of *Finn* is as much the story of *Woodface*.

Several songs initially written for this collaboration were used on the 1991 *Woodface* album. Tim Finn joined Crowded House and subsequently left the band mid-tour. It was good to see that the brothers' relationship was not overly harmed as a result of the experience.

The band was initially to be named Finn but was forced to become The Finn Brothers after another band with the same name took issue.

The issues surrounding band roles that were the cause of the problems with the *Woodface* years were not apparent on this album. There was an equal division of labour across the album, in terms of frontman, songwriting and playing. All instruments were played by Neil and Tim Finn, except for the bass, which was played by Dave Dobbyn.

For an album that was stripped of great songs such as 'There Goes God', 'It's Only Natural', 'Weather with You' and 'Four Seasons In One Day', it does not suffer in terms of quality. Given the talents of Neil and Tim Finn, the solution seemed to be just to write some more great tunes. Which they have. It is an album with a lot of charm; the pick of the bunch includes 'Only Talking Sense', 'Last Day of June', 'Suffer Never' and 'Angel's Heap'. The latter two songs were released as singles.

The album was produced by Tchad Blake, Neil Finn and Tim Finn, recorded and mixed at York St Studios, Auckland, in November 1994 and March 1995.

The original album was released on CD in November 1995 by Parlophone/Discovery. It was then rereleased in July 2022 on Pete Paphides' Needle Mythology label as a two-disc LP. A two-disc CD edition followed in November 2023 (Needle Mythology). The release included demos of a number of the songs that did not make *Finn* or *Woodface*. A version of 'Strangeness and Charm' can be found on Tim Finn's solo album.

The album did well on the charts, making the top twenty, in Australia, New Zealand and the UK. It also went down well with critics. The Times' Caitlin Moran said 'the album is bizarrely fractured [with] Astral Weeks-like drifts, underwater lullabies and melodies nicked from the Walkmans of the gods'.[1]

The album cover features a painting done by Neil Finn.

Tracklist

Original Album (1995)

'Only Talking Sense', 'Eyes of the World', 'Mood Swinging Man', 'Last Day of June', 'Suffer Never', 'Angel's Heap', 'Niwhai', 'Where Is My Soul', 'Bullets in My Hairdo', 'Paradise (Wherever You Are)', 'Kiss the Road of Rarotonga'.

2022/2023 Bonus Disc

'Catherine Wheels' (demo), 'Prodigal Son' (demo), 'Four-Stepping In 3/4 Time' (demo—previously unreleased), 'There Goes God' (demo), 'It's Only Natural' (demo), 'Weather With You' (demo), 'Strangeness And Charm' (demo), 'Four Seasons In One Day' (demo),
'In Love with It All' (demo), 'How Will You Go' (demo)

II. Neil Finn—*Try Whistling This* (1998)

Original album release:	June 1998 (Parlophone/Work)
Personnel:	Neil Finn: vocals, guitar and piano Tony Allen: drums Michael Barker: drums and percussion Lyn Buchannan: additional drums Marius De Vries: programming and keyboards Liam Finn: drums and guitar Paddy Free: programming Mitchell Froom: Hammond organ Jim Moginie: guitars,omnichord and percussion Robert Moore: bass Sebastian Steinberg: bass Pete Thomas: drums
Recorded at:	Looking Glass Studios, NYC (Nov–Dec 1997); Roundhead Studios, Auckland (May–Aug 1997). Additional recording at: Shelter Island Sound, NYC (Oct 1997); York Street Studios, Auckland (Oct 1996); Greenstone Studios, Karekare (Nov 1995)
Duration:	54:44
Produced by:	Neil Finn and Marius de Vries, except 'Try Whistling This', 'Truth' and Astro, produced by Neil Finn, 'Last One Standing' and 'Faster Than Light', produced by Neil Finn and Tchad Blake, and 'Addicted', produced by Neil Finn and Jim Moginie
Chart positions:	Australia: 1; New Zealand: 1; UK: 5

Having finished with his Crowded House commitments, Neil Finn felt it was time to start work on his first solo album. Songs written for Crowded House were put to one side for the time being. One of the motivating factors for moving on from Crowded House was that he felt he had written some songs did not suit his old band.

The recording needed a different approach. The album initially started in Finn's house in New Zealand. His home studio was being built at the time, so he utilised other rooms across the house to record the album, trying to stay out of the way of the builders in the process. The spark and the energy of the album is said to come from the time when Neil decamped to New York to finish the album.

All the songs were written by Neil Finn, except 'King Tide' (Neil Finn and Robert Moore), 'Try Whistling This', 'Loose Tongue' and 'Truth' (Neil Finn and Jim Moginie), and 'Sinner' (Neil Finn and Marius De Vries).

The album is still big on Neil Finn's trademark melodies and harmonies. The songwriting palette has been developed with more textures. There is nothing on the album that would scare off the diehard Crowded House fanbase. It is interesting to guess how this album would have sounded as a record by Crowded House.

'Try Whistling This', which is the pick of the bunch, is hard to see fitting with Crowded House's first phase. 'Souvenir' too is another highlight and features a song that started from a jam with Neil and his then 14-year-old son Liam. The singles 'She Will Have Her Way' and 'Last One Standing' are both radio-friendly numbers.

The album was produced by Neil Finn at various stages, with additional help from Marius de Vries, Tchad Blake, and Jim Moginie. It was recorded at Looking Glass Studios, New York City (November/December 1997) and at Roundhead Studios, Auckland (May–August 1997). The cover art came from a painting by Elroy Finn.

The reviews were generally positive for the album. XSNoise said, 'no matter what musical role Neil Finn would morph into, band member, partner, or soloist, he would always retain the singular ability to write outstanding and engaging musical works'.[2]

The album topped the charts in Australia and New Zealand and reached number five in the UK.

Original Album 1998

'Last One Standing', 'Souvenir', 'King Tide', 'Try Whistling This', 'She Will Have Her Way', 'Sinner', 'Twisty Bass', 'Loose Tongue', 'Truth', 'Astro',' Dream Date', 'Faster Than Light', 'Addicted'.

Australian edition bonus disc*

'Tokyo', 'Family Ties', 'She Comes Scattered', 'Identical Twin', '808 Song', 'Log Drums'.

*Some of these songs have appeared as extra tracks on the singles from the album.

III. Neil Finn—*One Nil* (2001)

Original album release:	March 2001 (Parlophone/EMI)
Personnel:	Neil Finn: guitar,vocals,high bass,piano,guitar synthesiser, orchestra bells,Wurlitzer electric piano,vibes,harmonium,bass and Chamberlin strings Wendy Melvoin: e-bow fuzz guitar, chorus on 'The Climber', drums, low bass, guitar, bass, percussion, backing vocals and shaker Jim Moginie: ukulele, guitar and fuzz guitar Lisa Germano: chorus on 'The Climber' and violin Suzanna Melvoin: chorus on 'The Climber' Doyle: chorus on 'The Climber' Tchad Blake: groove box Mitchell Froom: Penny Owsley, keyboards, Hammond organ, Chamberlin, Wurlitzer electric piano, piano and celeste Lisa Coleman: keyboards and backing vocals J. J. Johnson: drums Liam Finn: backing vocals Sharon Finn: backing vocals Jim Keltner: drums Edmund McWilliams: backing vocals Sheryl Crow: vocals and accordion Sam Gibson: drum programming and programming
Recorded at:	Roundhead Studios, Auckland and Sunset Sound Factory, Los Angeles, between June and December 1999, except 'Hole In the Ice', recorded at Revolver Studios, Auckland, June 2000
Duration:	48:46
Produced by:	Tchad Blake and Neil Finn, except 'Wherever You Are', produced by Tchad Blake, Mitchell Froom and Neil Finn
Chart positions:	Australia: 9; New Zealand: 29

After the elaborately textured debut solo album, came the second solo album *One Nil*. The sound is largely acoustic, and some of the songs would not sound out of place on The Finn Brothers releases.

Neil Finn was joined on the album by Lisa Coleman, and Wendy Melvoin, who have worked with Prince and under their own guise as Wendy & Lisa. Finn believed the album was more coherent than the previous release:

> This album, probably more so than the last one, has a thread that runs through it that's more consistent—partly because I had a steady collaborator in Wendy

> Melvoin, and I had the presence of other musicians right from the very beginning, which gave it a sound from the beginning.[3]

For Crowded House fans who may not take to the experimental nature of the first solo album would have enjoyed the back-to-basics approach that the album took. 'Wherever You Are' blends an organic Crowded House-like sound with an experimental, textured background. This song works well in this context, but it is still an exceptional pop song stripped of its adornments when played acoustically.

Other musicians who were on the album included Sheryl Crow, Lisa Germano and Jim Keltner on drums. All the songs were written by Neil Finn, apart from 'Rest Of The Day Off', which was co-written by Neil Finn, Wendy Melvoin and Tchad Blake, 'Hole In the Ice', by Neil Finn and Lisa Coleman, and 'Last To Know and Don't Ask Why', by Neil Finn and Wendy Melvoin.

Neil Finn has nothing but praise for Melvoin's contributions to the album: 'Wendy's feel on "Don't Ask Why" is just a joy to play with. It was a different feel than I'd ever worked with before.'[4]

All songs produced by Tchad Blake and Neil Finn apart from 'Wherever You Are'; this sees Mitchell Froom back producing a Neil Finn album. This was the first time the pair had worked together since they recorded the extra tracks on the *Recurring Dream* compilation album.

The album is dedicated to Neil Finn's mother, Mary, who died during the making of the album.

Tracklist

'The Climber', 'Rest of The Day Off', 'Hole In The Ice', 'Wherever You Are', 'Last To Know', 'Don't Ask Why', 'Secret God', 'Turn and Run', 'Elastic Heart', 'Anytime', 'Driving Me Mad', 'Into The Sunset'.

IV: Various—*Rain* (Soundtrack)

Original album release: October 2001

This was Neil Finn's first foray into writing soundtrack material for *Rain*, a 2001 New Zealand film directed by Christine Jeffs. It is based on the novel of the same name written by Kirsty Gunn. It is a coming-of-age tale of 13-year-old Janey. He says: 'I was lucky to have a dark, atmospheric piece to bring all my moody instrumental music out of the closet.'[5]

It was good to bring out this aspect of his songwriting for the collection; it was a good one.

The reviews were quite positive. One described it as '...an effective freshman film music outing, one that makes me hope Neil Finn might try this again sometime'.[6]

Apart from the odd excursion here and there into soundtrack work, I am surprised there have not been many more full-scale commissions like this one.

Tracklist

'You Don't Know'—Neil Finn (song), 'Summer Intro'—Neil Finn (score), 'Summer Of Love'—Neil Finn and Edmund McWilliams (song), 'Mum In Bed'—Neil Finn (score), 'Orange And Blue'—Neil Finn (song), 'Red Room'—Neil Finn (score), 'Cry Wolf'—Lisa Germano (song), 'The Affair'—Neil Finn (score), 'Black Sally'—Human Instinct (song), 'Boat Dawn'—Neil Finn (score), 'Boat Joyride'—Neil Finn (song), 'Kids Floating'—Neil Finn (score), 'Batman'—Neil Finn (score), 'Shower'—Neil Finn (score), 'Phantom Love'—Lisa Germano (score), 'Drive Home'—Neil Finn and Edmund McWilliams (song) 'Lucid Dream'—Liam Finn (song).

V. Various—*7 Worlds Collide (Live at The St. James)*

CD & DVD release:	November 2001 (Parlophone/Nettwerk)
Personnel:	Neil Finn: vocals, electric guitar, acoustic guitar and acoustic twelve-string guitar Tim Finn: vocals, acoustic guitar and piano Ed O'Brien: vocals, electric guitar, e-bow, acoustic guitar and effects Johnny Marr: vocals, electric guitar, ukulele and acoustic guitar Lisa Germano: vocals, keyboard, piano, violin, electric guitar and ukulele Sebastian Steinberg: bass, electric bass and double bass Phil Selway: drums Eddie Vedder: vocals, electric guitar and ukulele Paul Jeffery: keyboard and organ Liam Finn: electric guitar Chris Garland: electric guitar Joe Bramley: bass Matt Eccles: drums
Recorded live at:	St James Theatre, Auckland, New Zealand, 2–6 April 2001 by Sam Gibson, assisted by Sean Craig
Mixed by:	Bob Clearmountain, assisted by Kevin Harp and Sam Gibson
Duration:	74:44

The album is credited as Neil Finn and Friends. It is good when you can call on friends like Ed O'Brien and Phil Selway from Radiohead, Johnny Marr, Pearl Jam's Eddie Vedder. Sebastian Steinberg and Lisa Germano, along with brother Tim, Liam Finn and his band Betchadupa. Given the stellar line-up, the project that emerges had every chance of success. The name for the project was derived from the line in the 1993 Crowded House song 'Distant Sun'.

The album features several live recordings of songs by Neil Finn, Crowded House, Split Enz and The Finn Brothers. It came about by chance when Neil Finn met Radiohead's Ed O'Brien on holiday:

> You meet people briefly, and you have a little exchange, and it's real nice and often people go, 'It'll be great to do something together, someday,' and it never happens. We went, 'Well, maybe we should just set up a couple of shows and ring up a few people that we've met and see if they want to come and do a collective. 'As it turned out, I had just met Johnny Marr at the Royal Albert Hall. We'd done a benefit for Linda McCartney. I rang him and it came at a good time for him. He was in between things, and he thought it sounded romantic and wonderful and said 'Yep!' straightaway. I rang Eddie and he was in Hawaii at the time and said, 'You want to come and do this thing? You can think about it; let me know.' And he went, 'No, no, I'm in.' Straightaway. 'Yeah, I'll come.' I went, 'Okay, well, but just give it some thought.' [*Laughs.*] I didn't believe that he could decide that easily. But it was just remarkably easy to organise as it turned out.[7]

Eddie Vedder steals the show with his contributions on 'Stuff and Nonsense'. Johnny Marr and Neil Finn's take on The Smiths' 'There is a Light That'll Never Go Out' is also a standout. This is something that they have often performed together live at various gigs over the years.

7 Worlds Collide: Live at the St. James was released in 2001. It was recorded at the St James Theatre in Auckland, New Zealand, 2–6 April 2001.

A CD and DVD were released in November 2001 on Parlophone and Nettwerk. The DVD contains more of the tracks from the gigs that did not appear on the CD.

Tracklist

'Fall At Your Feet'(DVD only), 'Anytime', 'Hole In The Ice'(DVD only), 'Paper Doll', 'The Climber', 'Take A Walk', 'Last To Know' (DVD only), 'Down On The Corner', 'There Is A Light That Never Goes Out', 'Private Universe' (DVD only), 'Parting Ways', 'Driving Me Mad' (DVD only), 'Turn and Run', 'Loose Tongue', 'She Will Have Her Way', 'Angel's Heap', 'Edible Flowers', 'Stuff And Nonsense', 'Four Seasons in One Day' (DVD only), 'Suffer Never' (DVD only), 'Cry Wolf' (DVD only), 'History Never Repeats' (DVD only), 'I See Red', 'Paradise (Wherever You Are)', 'Weather With You', 'Don't Dream It's Over'.

VI. *One All*

CD release: November 2002 (Nettwerk America)
Personnel: as per the original *One Nil* album

Produced by:	Tchad Blake and Neil Finn, except 'Wherever You Are', produced by Tchad Blake, Mitchell Froom and Neil Finn, 'Human Kindness' and 'Lullabye Requiem', produced by Neil Finn, and 'Wherever You Are' produced by Tchad Blake, Mitchell Froom and Neil Finn
Recorded at:	Roundhead Studios, Auckland and Sunset Sound Factory, Los Angeles between June and December 1999, except 'Hole In The Ice', recorded at Revolver Studios, Auckland, June 2000, and 'Human Kindness' and 'Lullaby Requiem',recorded at Roundhead Studios, October/November 2001
Duration:	49:00

This is ostensibly the *One Nil* album; however, it has been reworked for the US market. It was released on the Nettwork America label. There is a differing track listing, featuring four remixed songs and new songs, including 'Lullaby Requiem', 'Human Kindness', replacing 'Elastic Heart' and 'Don't Ask Why'.

In particular, this version of 'Hole in the Ice' is noticeably different. The original was less polished; the newer version is slicker and has taken out the rougher edges.

The changes are something that Neil Finn endorsed. He was not under any record company pressure to do so, as he told the fan club newsletter in 2002:

> It's finally come around... I'm about to venture forth into the US with the album renamed, re-sequenced, remixed, refreshed and about time too. I hope you like the remodelled 'One All'. It felt important to me to improve a few aspects, having waited so long to see it come out.[8]

The album again contains a dedication to his mother Mary. 'Lullaby Requiem' has been added to this album and it is a perfect tribute to Neil Finn's mother.

Tracklist

'The Climber', 'Driving Me Mad', 'Last to Know', 'Wherever You Are', 'Secret God', 'Lullaby', 'Requiem', 'Human Kindness', 'Turn and Run', 'Anytime', 'Rest of The Day Off', 'Into The Sunset'.

VII. The Finn Brothers—*Everyone is Here*

Album release:	August 2004 (Parlophone/Nettwerk)
Personnel:	Neil Finn: vocals, guitars, piano, bass and string arrangements Tim Finn: vocals, piano, percussion, tambourine, Hammond organ and string arrangements

	Sebastian Steinberg: bass Mitchell Froom: piano, Schill piano, organ, orchestron and Wurlitzer Matt Chamberlain drums Pete Thomas: drums Jon Brion: drum fills, percussion, guitar, Turkish bajo, twelve-string guitar, organ, tuned drums, percussion loops, acoustic guitar, face percussion and harmonium Dave Faragher: bass B. J. Cole: pedal steel Don McGlashan: euphonium Neil Watson: lap steel James Crabb: accordion Tony Visconti: string arrangements, double bass, mandolin and throat singing Geoff Maddock: string arrangements
Recorded at:	Cello Studios, Hollywood, February–March 2004 by Adam Kaspar, assisted by Steven Rhodes. Additional recording at Sage and Sound Recording Studio, Hollywood.
Engineered by:	Steven Rhodes, assisted by Errin Familia.
Album completed at:	The Unknown Falls in April 2004, engineered by David Boucher. Additional recording at Roundhead Studios, Auckland, engineered by Neil Baldock. 'Disembodied Voices' recorded at Allaire Studios, Shokan, NY, by Tony Visconti and Mario McNulty, assisted by Mark McKenna and Matthew Cullen, London by Chris Dibble
Duration:	45:47
Produced by:	The Finn Brothers and Mitchell Froom. Except 'Gentle Hum' which is produced by Neil Finn and Jon Brion; 'Luckiest Man Alive' produced by The Finn Brothers, Jon Brion and Mitchell Froom; 'Disembodied Voices' produced by Tony Visconti and The Finn Brothers

The second album from The Finn Brothers sees them going for a more lavish production. The last album has a rustic, low-fi charm; this time, they have looked at producing something with a more polished sound.

The album was primarily produced by The Finn Brothers and Mitchell Froom but also features production contributions from Jon Brion and Tony Visconti.

Neil Finn was happy with the results of the production:

> A brilliant cast of characters involved from Tony Visconti, Adam Kasper, Mitchell Froom, Jon Brion, Bob Clearmountain, with good old school A&R support Chris Briggs on hand… sounded effortless in the end… that's the art![9]

The album was recorded in various studios in Hollywood and New York in spring 2004 with the usual additional recording back home at Roundhead Studios, Auckland.

All songs were co-written by the brothers, apart from 'All The Colours' and 'The Gentle Hum,' which written by Neil. 'Edible Flowers' —an unreleased Split Enz song written during recording sessions in August 1999 in the lead-up to the Enz of the Millennium concerts—was written by Tim Finn, Neil Finn, Noel Crombie, Nigel Griggs and Eddie Rayner.

For Tim Finn, the song highlights the skills both brothers bring to the songwriting process:

> Neil's very good at going somewhere that I would never have thought of. One example is 'Edible Flowers'. I had an idea for a verse and had some lyrics, but I would never have taken it where Neil took it, which is the uplifting, bittersweet chorus that followed.[10]

The highlight of the collection is 'Won't Give In' along with Edible Flowers. It is a solid set of songs, probably lacking in terms of the consistency that their previous album had.

The cover photo is of Neil and Tim Finn taken at the Waikato River between Te Awamutu and Auckland, New Zealand.

Tracklist

'Won't Give In', 'Nothing Wrong With You', 'Anything Can Happen', 'Luckiest Man Alive', 'Homesick', 'Disembodied Voices', 'A Life Between Us', 'All God's Children', 'Edible Flowers', 'All The Colours', 'Part Of Me Part Of You', 'Gentle Hum'

VIII. Various—*7 Worlds Collide—Sun Came Out*

Original album release:	August 2009 (Sony Music / Oxfam) (1-CD, 2-CD and 2-LP editions)
Documentary by:	Republic Films released on DVD in 2012 Concert film released digitally in February 2019
Personnel:	Neil Finn, Johnny Marr, Ed O'Brien, Phil Selway, Sebastian Steinberg, Lisa Germano, Liam Finn, Bic Runga, Don McGlashan, K. T. Tunstall, Jeff Tweedy, Spencer Tweedy, John Stirratt, Pat Sansone, Glenn Kotche, Glenn Richards, Tim Finn Album project produced by Jim Scott and Neil Finn. Additional production by Neil Baldock in Studio B
Engineered by:	Jim Scott, Neil Baldock, Jordan Stone and Simon Gooding, assisted by Dave Paul

All tracks recorded at Roundhead Studios, Auckland, NZ, Christmas 2008 and January 2009
Duration: 1 CD: 53:03 2 CD: 94:02
Charts: Australian: 39; New Zealand: 2

Following on from the success of the *7 Worlds Collide* live album, came the follow-up. The easiest way might have been to have put together another live concert, but given the songwriting talents gathered last time, maybe an album of original material was inevitable.

Again, it was the brainchild of Neil Finn. He managed to corral a group of musicians to his Roundhead Studios in New Zealand. A number of those who got involved in the 2001 project signed up again, these included Johnny Marr, Ed O'Brien, Phil Selway, Sebastian Steinberg, Lisa Germano, Tim Finn and Liam Finn. Recruits for this album included Don McGlashan, Bic Runga, Glenn Richards and KT Tunstall, as well as the American alt-rockers Wilco, including members Jeff Tweedy, John Stirratt, Glenn Kotche and Pat Sansone.

Wilco bassist John Stirratt said:

> Neil Finn came to us backstage when we were playing in Chicago in 2008 and he had just had the idea of doing another *7 Worlds Collide* and invited us. I think he got introduced to the band through his kids, and that's how he got turned on to Wilco and how he thought we would be a good fit for the *7 Worlds Collide* project. It was wonderful, Neil was amazing; there are not many guys who can oversee a project like that. First of all, he owns a studio that has three functioning rooms in it with all the stuff. Not many people could have done that, and Neil is one and maybe (Paul) McCartney would be the other guy who could maybe do something like that.[11]

Wilco enjoyed the experience so much they stayed on a recorded their 2009 album, *Wilco (the album)* at Neil Finn's Roundhead Studios.

Although this is not a Neil Finn or Crowded House record, it is Finn who is the strand that is running through this. Whether that be performing on a track or producing the album. There are several notable songwriting contributions along the way. 'Little by Little' is a preview of what was to come with the *Pyjama Club* album from Neil and Sharon Finn. It is a good introduction to that project. Ed O'Brien and Neil Finn's 'Bodhisattva Blues' is a rocky number. Neil's 'All Comedians suffer' is a great collaborative effort with Liam Finn and Wilco.

As a charity project, it is already a success in the fact that it gathered together people to raise money for Oxfam. From a creative point of view, the project gathered together many great artists to record a collection that stands together quite well.

The album was produced by Jim Scott and Neil Finn with additional production by Neil Baldock.

The Sun Came Out was released in August 2009 by Sony Music/Oxfam. There were several editions available: a two-disc CD version and a single disc version.

It was also available on vinyl. A documentary of the project was released by Republic Films on DVD in 2012. A concert film was releaseddigitally in February 2019.

Tracklist

Disc 1

'Too Blue'(Johnny Marr and Jeff Tweedy), 'You Never Know'(Jeff Tweedy), 'Little By Little' (Sharon Finn and Neil Finn), 'Learn To Crawl' (Ed O'Brien, Johnny Marr, Liam Finn, and Neil Finn), 'Black Silk Ribbon'(KT Tunstall and Bic Runga), 'Girl, Make Your Own Mind Up'(Don McGlashan), 'Run In The Dust'(Johnny Marr), 'Red Wine Bottle'(Liam Finn, Chris Garland, and Johnny Marr), 'The Ties That Bind Us'(Phil Selway), 'Reptile'(Lisa Germano), 'Bodhisattva Blues' (Ed O'Brien and Liam Finn), 'What Could Have Been' (Jeff Tweedy)

Disc 2

'All Comedians Suffer'(Neil Finn), 'Duxton Blues'(Glenn Richards), 'Hazel Black'(KT Tunstall and Neil Finn), 'Riding The Wave'(Tim Finn), 'The Witching Hour'(Phil Selway), 'Over And Done' (John Stirratt), 'A Change Of Heart'(Bic Runga and Dan Wilson), 'Don't Forget Me'(Pat Sansone), 'Long Time Gone'(Don McGlashan), 'The Cobbler'(Elroy Finn), 3 Worlds Collide (Glenn Kotche, Phil Selway, and Neil Baldock), 'The Water'(Sebastian Stein)

IX. Pajama Club—*Pajama Club*

Original album release:	September 2011
Personnel:	Sharon Finn:vocals, bass
	Neil Finn: vocals, drums, guitars, keyboards
	Sean Donnelly: synthesisers, noises, backing vocals
Produced by:	Sean Donnelly and Neil Finn
Duration:	43:29

Sharon Finn's name can be found on several Crowded House releases down the years, mainly on backing vocals. She stepped from the shadows on the track 'Isolation', on the *Intriguer* album, so brilliantly. This may have been the push that she needed to step further forward.

The billing on the liner notes for the album intentionally has Neil Finn listed after his wife. The Pajama Club is a side project that came about when husband and wife found themselves jamming in the music room after their sons, Liam and Elroy, had left home. The empty nesters put their newfound time together to create this album.

'Tell Me What You Want' pushes Sharon's bass guitar to the fore. Neil Finn plays drums to good effect. For someone whohas disparaged his skills as adrummer over the years, he does a great job behind the kit on this one. It shows the bass-and-drum (as opposed to drum 'n' bass) focus of the album. There are many electronic textures throughout. There are hints of Talking Heads and Tom Tom Club about this album, not just the collaboration of a husband-and-wife rhythm section.

'From A Friend to A Friend' was one of the tracks chosen as the lead single on the album; again, it has the band's distinct sound. Despite the electronic flourishes, Finn's gift for melody is still there.

Sean Donnelly was the other member of the band on synthesisers, noises, and backing vocals. He also collaborated on the writing of several of the songs

The band did step out of the music room to perform live on a string of dates. They were joined by drummer Alana Skyring (formerly of The Grates) to enable Neil Finn to step forward.

This is a great album, one that may have been forgotten about over time. Surprisingly, they have not followed this up at any point in the last few years.

Tracklist

'Tell Me What You Want', 'Can't Put It Down Until It Ends', 'These Are Conditions', 'From A Friend to A Friend', 'Golden Child', 'Daylight', 'Go Kart', 'Dead Leg', 'TNT For 2', 'The Game We Love To Play', 'Diamonds In Her Eyes; bonus track (iTunes/Apple Music): 'Suffer Never'/'Are Friends Electric'.

X. Neil Finn And Paul Kelly—*Goin' Your Way (Live)*

2CD, DVD, Blu-ray and Deluxe Edition release in November 2013 (EMI)
2CD released in the US in December 2015 (Omnivore)
Highlights vinyl LP released on Record Store Day in November 2015 (Omnivore)

Personnel:	Neil Finn: guitars, piano, keyboards and vocals Paul Kelly guitars, piano, keyboards, percussion and vocals Elroy Finn: drums, acoustic guitar and backing vocals Dan Kelly: guitars and backing vocals Zoe Hauptmann: double bass, bass guitar and backing vocals
Duration:	119:58
Recorded in:	Sydney on Monday 18 March 2013
Executive producers:	Bill Cullen and Micheal Bradshaw
Set design and cover art:	Noel Crombie and Sally-Anne Mills
Charts:	Australia: 5

Following on from the *7 Worlds Collide* collaboration, this potential match-up was often talked about but took some time in coming together.

It finally happened in February and March 2013 as the two longstanding friends, Neil Finn and Paul Kelly, toured together, reinterpreting songs from both their illustrious catalogues. The album that came out was recorded on 10 March 2013 at the Sydney Opera House.

In the liner notes for the album, Paul Kelly said of the collaboration:

> Neil and I met in the mid-1980s and first played together when Crowded House toured America in 1987. My band opened up for them, and they would invite me up on stage during their set to sing 'Leaps and Bounds'. We had some good post-show singalongs on that trip and continued to cross paths over the years, sometimes on stages and sometimes on tennis courts. Despite long gaps between seeing each other, each time we met, there was an ease and companionability born, I suspect, out of similar upbringing and family backgrounds. We are both from close-knit Irish Catholic clans that like to get together to eat, drink and gossip. laugh and sing. It was that family feeling we wanted to bring to our shows.[12]

Neil said of the project:

> When Paul and I first discussed how we might approach this tour, we were both adamant that it had to be special, not enough to just turn up and take turns playing our songs with a hot session band and a few anecdotes. Something magic happens when you become a proper band. Everyone invests and gets emotionally involved. Elroy, Dan and Zoe were all beautifully prepared and gave so much of themselves to the process. We worked twelve-hour rehearsals in the sweaty confines of rehearsal rooms and left feeling excited every day.[13]

'For the Ages' shows the collaborative process coming together quite well in the live setting, with Paul and Dan Kelly's song faultlessly performed. Several Neil Finn and Crowded House songs sound great performed in this style.

The pair were joined by Elroy Finn, on drums, acoustic guitar and backing vocals. Making it a family affair, Paul's nephew Dan added guitars and backing vocals. Zoe Hauptmann augmented the band on double bass, bass guitar and backing vocals.

The handmade backdrop for the gigs was made by Noel Crombie and Sally Mills. It was also recreated as the cover art for the album.

The album has been released in numerous formats. A 2CD, DVD, Blu-ray and Deluxe Edition was released 8 November 2013, on EMI. A 2CD version was released in the US on 11 December 2015 by Omnivore. A highlights version was released for Record Store Day on 27 November 2015 by Omnivore.

Tracklist

Disc 1

'Don't Stand So Close to the Window', 'Four Seasons In One Day', 'Before Too Long', 'She Will Have Her Way', 'Not The Girl You Think You Are', 'For The

Ages', 'Sinner', 'Won't Give In', 'Careless, 'Leaps And Bounds', 'Only Talking Sense', 'New Found Year', 'Into Temptation', 'You Can Put Your Shoes Under My Bed', 'Private Universe'

Disc 2
'Dumb Things', 'One Step Ahead', 'Deeper Water', 'Better Be Home Soon', 'How to Make Gravy', 'Distant Sun', 'Winter Coat', 'Fall At Your Feet', 'To Her Door', 'Don't Dream It's Over', 'Message To My Girl', 'Love Is The Law', 'Words Of Love', 'Moon River'.

XI. Neil Finn—*Dizzy Heights*

Original album release: February 2014 (Lester Records/Kobalt)
Personnel: Neil Finn: guitar, lead vocals, clarinet, drums, keyboards, synthesiser, vibraphone and producer
Liam Finn: guitar, percussion, backing vocals and producer
Sharon Finn: bass and backing vocals
Elroy Finn: drums and backing vocals
Victoria Kelly: string arrangements
Glenn Kotche: body percussion
Ashley Brown: cello
Matt Chamberlain: drums
Sean Donnelly: electronic drums and backing vocals
Dave Fridmann: engineer and producer
Will Ricketts: percussion
Aarahdna: backing vocals
Madeleine Sami: backing vocals
Mary Fridmann: backing vocals
Benjamin Knapp:whistling
Duration: 46:54
Recorded at: Tarbox Studios, Buffalo and Roundhead Studios, Auckland
Produced by: Dave Fridmann and Neil Finn
Engineered by: David Fridmann, assisted by Andrew Everding
Additional engineering at: Roundhead Studios by Jordan Stone, Benjamin Knapp, Jason Huss, Neil Baldock
Mixed by: Dave Fridmann at Tarbox Studios
Mastered by: Greg Calbi, assisted by Steve Fallone at Sterling Sound, NYC
Artwork by: Gideon Keith, cover image by Neil Finn

After a few interesting diversions, both as extended solo projects and with Crowded House, it was back to putting out another Neil Finn record. For this one, he called on the services of Dave Fridmann, formerly of Mercury Rev and The Flaming Lips, to help produce the record. It is the third Neil Finn solo record, the follow-up to *One Nil/One All*. It is a slickly produced affair. These days, it is hard to second-guess the type of album Neil Finn will release, given his fondness for not doing something too obvious.

The album includes several people that Finn has worked with on recent projects. The lead single, 'Flying In the Face of Love', has writing credits from Neil Finn, Sharon Finn and Sean Donnelly. This sounds like a song that could have been on their *Pajama Club* album. The bass and the atmospherics are reminiscent of that album. Neil, Sharon, Elroy and Liam all appear on 'Pony Ride', another strong number from the collection. These are probably the most radio-friendly songs amongst the selection.

'Divebomber' is another dreamy number that wears the influences of the producer quite closely. 'Strangest of Friends' can also be found on the bonus disc of the 2016 *Intriguer* Deluxe Edition of the album, tucked away on a song called 'Nonsense of Course', which gathered together studio jams. 'Pony Ride' is said to be his dad's favourite song on the album.

It is a good, solid album.

Again, Neil Finn is not afraid to mix up the sonic palette of his songs. This album has a sheen on it that had not been heard before. Elements of this sound can be heard on many of the subsequent releases. It is probably one that would not have found much favour beyond the Crowded House diehards.

It was recorded at Tarbox Studios, Buffalo and Roundhead Studios, Auckland. The album was released on 7 February 2014 by Lester Records/Kobalt.

Tracklist

'Impressions', 'Dizzy Heights', 'Flying In The Face Of Love', 'Divebomber', 'Better Than TV', 'Pony Ride', 'White Lies and Alibis', 'Recluse', 'Strangest Friends', 'In My Blood', 'Lights of New York'; bonus tracks: 'Animal vs Human', 'Your Next Move'.

XII. Neil Finn—*Out of Silence* 2017

Recorded 25 August 2017. Released 1 September 2017 (Lester Records/ Universal)

Personnel:
Neil Finn: vocal, piano and string composition
Tim Finn: vocal and guitar (on 'Alone')
Elroy Finn: bass, guitar and drum programming
Liam Finn: drums and drum programming
The Infinity Orchestra: strings

	Victoria Kelly: conductor, orchestra arrangements and string composition
	E. J. Barnes, Sean Donnelly, Harper Finn, Reb Fountain, Hollie Fullbrook, Victoria Kelly, Don McGlashan, Jimmy Metherell, Sandy Mill, James Milne, Amelia Murray and Samuel Flynn Scott: choir
	David Squire: choir director
	Simon Gooding: drum programming
Duration:	36:00
Produced by:	Neil Finn and Liam Finn

According to Stephen King, a writer should 'write with the door closed, rewrite with the door open'.[14] For *Out of Silence*, the door was well and truly open for all aspects of putting the album together.

In August 2027, Neil Finn provided an insight into his creative process by allowing fans to follow the progress of his new album, *Out of Silence*, as it was written, rehearsed and recorded. The sessions would also throw in a couple of old favourites into the mix to get the creative juices flowing.

Neil Finn said in the lead up to the project:

> During these Friday sessions, you will be witness to a series of musical happenings featuring friends, family, fellow songwriters and singers playing tunes both old and brand new. You can follow the progress of new song arrangements as we build towards the last stream on August 25. This final performance will be the actual recording of my new solo album.[15]

Out of Silence emerged from four weekly Friday live streams, with a final four-hour session concluding the process. The recording, which took place on 25 August 2017, saw a quick turnaround, with the album being released on1 September 2017.

The first session saw the recording of 'More Than One Of You', which was released digitally. They did about four takes, and they fashioned something that they could release on the album.

The album is a sumptuously produced record. No half-measures were taken; it would no doubt have been easier to release something stripped-back and lo-fi. The album that emerged from the sessions was far from being undercooked.

For Neil, that was important:

> For a long time, I've wanted to do a record in one crack and get it out in a week... Then I thought, 'Well, if we're going to do that, let's not make it a little acoustic thing that's easy to record in one session. Let's make it the most sophisticated record I've ever made.[16]

'Chameleon Days' has a beautiful mix of piano and choir. Neil employs a whispered falsetto vocal for the verse. It is a beautifully realised song. 'Independence Day' too. Neil and Tim Finn combine well for 'Alone'. It is wonderfully evocative. The beautiful harmonies ring out with a rainy day feel.

At times, the album feels like a film score. It is a very introspective album. 'Second Nature' is the only up-tempo song, which was released as a digital single to promote the album.

It is another album where Neil Finn has tried to mix it up a little. Anyone trying to second-guess the next steps is likely to be proved wrong.

Tracklist

'Love is Emotional', 'More Than One Of You', 'Chameleon Days', 'Independence Day', 'Alone', 'Widow's Peak', 'Second Nature', 'The Law Is Always On Your Side', 'Terrorise Me', 'I Know Different'

XIII: Neil Finn and Liam Finn—*Lightsleeper*

Original album release: August 2018 (Inertia/PIAS)
Personnel: Neil Finn: vocals, piano, Wurlitzer, acoustic guitar, electric guitar, bass, ARP strings, synth, slide guitar, Mellotron, beats, drum synthesiser and drums
Liam Finn: vocals, electric guitar, bass, beats, drums, acoustic guitar, synth, sound effects samples and loops
Elroy Finn: drums, percussion and slide guitar
Sharon Finn: bass and vocals
Mick Fleetwood: drums and percussion
Connan Mockasin: electric guitar and choir
Elias Dendias: bouzouki
Spiros Anemogianis: accordion
Barnes Family: choir
Devo Finns: choir
Jimmy Metherrell: choir
Elliot Finn: vocals
Harper Finn: whisper
Matthew Eccles: percussion
Kody Nielson: drums
Victoria Kelly: string arrangements
Duration: 48:57
Produced by: Neil Finn, Liam Finn and Tchad Blake
Recorded by: Tchad Blake, Liam Finn and Neil Finn
Orchestra recorded by: Jordan Stone
Additional engineering: Scott Seabright, Jordan Stone, Paddy Hill and Kody Neilson

Recorded at:	Roundhead Studios
Mastered at:	Gateway Mastering by Bob Ludwig
Additional recordings at:	ThonicPeenith studios LA and Studio C, Greece
Mixed at:	Mongrel Studios by Tchad Blake, except Troubles and Hold Her Close mixed by Liam Finn
Additional engineers:	Scott Seabright, Ben Malone, Paddy Hill
Cover by:	Liam Finn. Art and design Dave Homer

The album is a family affair in more ways than one. It is the wedding album that celebrates Liam Finn's marriage. The songwriting is shared across the family, too.

It is 2015 and Liam Finn was to marry his partner, Janina, on a Greek island. Liam's father, Neil Finn, has done what one would expect one of the greatest songwriters of his generation to do, in the event of his songwriting son getting married: he has written a new song for the occasion. It is debuted at the point in the wedding when everyone has been invited to do some 'free expression dancing', said the writer Caitlin Moran at the time of the release of the album.[17]

Neil and Liam work well together, although Neil was worried on some level that it might not work out. Neil admits:

> It was risky, as we are both quite stubborn and pedantic about different things. I was worried we might clash and expose some weird, deep family anxiety—but in fact we just upped the patience, tolerance and respect quotient, and avoided most of the angst.[18]

For Liam, he relished the chance to work with his dad.

> I love dad's music. I've grown up with it being such a huge part of my life—I know it like the back of my hand. It's been great to have him learn my songs and see his appreciation for what I do.[19]

The album was produced by Neil and Liam Finn, along with long-time associate Tchad Blake. It was recorded in Neil's Roundhead Studios. Added to the family mix of the musicians performing on the album is long-term string arranger Victoria Kelly and the notable presence of Mick Fleetwood.

'Where's My Room' is an interesting song. It manages to singlehandedly distil the feel of the album, starting off with an approximation of Beck and Prince before diverting into something symphonic and closing with a straightforward song.

'We Know What It Means' reads like a father-to-son discussion about the days of growing up on the road. The arrangement is reminiscent of the songs that John Lennon wrote when he was living a relatively secluded life in New York in the late 1970s.

The album is a mix of lo-fi sounds and atmospherics. The songs sound experimental and unconventional at times. Some of these ideas feel like they would have been more fully realised if Crowded House had recorded them. As an album it is an interesting diversion, one for the Crowded House completists maybe, but not an album to gain new followers.

Tracklist

'Prelude—Island Of Peace', 'Meet Me In The Air', 'Where's My Room', 'Anger Plays A Part', 'Listen', 'Any Other Way', 'Back to Life', 'Hiding Place', 'Ghosts', 'We Know What It Means', 'Hold Her Close'; bonus track on vinyl edition: 'Troubles'

XIV. Neil Finn—*Solo at The Seymour Centre, 2010*

Released: October 2020

Not just content to entertain fans of Crowded House with his excellent *Fangradio* sessions during the COVID lockdowns, Neil Finn also raised money for the road crew whose work had dried up as a result of lockdowns around the world.

He explained his reasoning for releasing this particular show now:

> I did a solo show at the Seymour Centre in Sydney ten years ago, which was one of the most enjoyable shows in memory. The good people at the Australian Road Crew Association asked me if I would make the desk tape recording available to raise money for the Support Act, a fund which benefits members of the live crew industry who have fallen on hard times or ill health. It couldn't be more timely to be thinking of the incredible people who are the backbone of our industry. It's been a tough year for them with no shows.[20]

The album was released online on 1 October 2020 (Black Box Records). There is a bit of a glitch in the concert recording and it starts at the beginning of the first chorus. To best represent the flow of the concert, the track is still included. It is a track list that covers all bases in the Finn repertoire, not just the Crowded House back catalogue.

Tracklist

'Only Talking Sense' (excerpt), 'Spirit of the Stairs', 'One Step Ahead', 'Hello Sandy Allen', 'Try, Whistling This', 'Wherever You Are', 'Last Day of June', 'Gentle Hum', 'Faster Than Light', 'Message To My Girl', 'Into The Sunset', 'Anytime', 'Love Is All That Remains', 'Something So Strong', 'She Will Have Her Way', 'Fall At Your Feet', 'Don't Dream It's Over'.

XV. Neil Finn—*Sessions at West 54th (Live)*

Broadcast: 13 September 1998
DVD release: December 2000
Limited edition vinyl release on Record Store Day, April 2025 (Legacy Recordings)
Digital audio stream release: 17 April 2025

The album started life as a broadcast for the 'Sessions at West 54th' series in the US. The performance was recorded in September 1998 and mostly has tracks from Finn's debut solo album as well as a few Crowded House numbers, plus 'I Got You' from Split Enz. It was initially released on DVD in 2000 but a limited-edition vinyl was released on Record Store Day on 12 April 2025 by Legacy Recordings. It was also available on digital platforms a week later.

The second series of the show was introduced by Talking Heads' David Byrne and his introduction can be heard on the record. The album is a good insight into the developing sound of Neil Finn as a solo artist. He was joined as a guest by his former colleague in Crowded House, Mark Hart. Liam Finn was also part of the band.

Tracklist

David Byrne intro, 'Try Whistling This', 'Addicted', 'Fall At Your Feet', 'Don't Dream It's Over', 'Twisty Bass', 'King Tide', 'I Got You', 'Astro', 'Faster Than Light', 'Loose Tongue', 'Souvenir', 'She Will Have Her Way', 'Truth', 'Last One Standing', 'Sinner'.

14

Selected Solo Tracks

Several Crowded House and Neil Finn tracks have been featured on several movie soundtracks; these are discussed on the pages that discuss the original albums and songs. The following songs are one-off collaborations and commissions that have not been included on Crowded House or solo albums. These are not singles per se, but additional releases that have popped up along the way.

'Song of a Lonely Mountain' (from *The Hobbit: An Unexpected Journey*)

Lyrics written by Neil Finn, music composed by Neil Finn, David Donaldson, David Long, Steve Roche and Janet Roddick
Duration: 6:01
Released on the original soundtrack in December 2012 (Decca)

It would be unthinkable if New Zealand's premier musical talent had played no part in any of Peter Jackson's movies from the *Lord of the Rings* franchise. This is not a score or a full soundtrack, but a song that can be found on the end credits of *The Hobbit: An Unexpected Journey* movie.

Neil Finn has said about his role on the soundtrack: 'I was asked to write new lyrics for and expand on a theme, sung by the dwarves, that appears early in *The Hobbit* movie. That theme was written by the good folk from Plan 9 and David Long in Wellington who have done previous soundtrack work on *Lord of the Rings*.'[1]

The song's folky overtones blend together well with the expansive soundtrack arrangement.

'Blue Smoke' (Anzac Day 2015) (Neil Finn and Jim Carter)

Written by Ruru Karaitiana
Duration: 2.45
Released as a single in April 2015 (Thom Music)

The song is a version of 'Blue Smoke', a track composed by Ruru Karaitiana in 1940. Neil Finn is joined on the song by Jim Carter who played steel guitar on the 1948 recording with singer Pixie Williams. The collaboration is a version of the first major musical hit from New Zealand. The song was released to commemorate the centenary of the Gallipoli landing.

Jim was in his late nineties at the time of the recording. There is a charming video of the pair meeting and working their way through the song.[2] Jim was modest about his talents and being able to get the track recorded. As can be heard on the record, they have managed to capture the essence of the original. It is a sparse recording that fits the authenticity of what they were trying to capture. The use of softly strummed guitar, ukuleles and lap steel guitars produces a brilliantly rendered cover version. The song on its own is worth a listen, but knowing the backstory makes the collaboration all the more heart-warming.

The song was released to raise funds to support the RSA's 2015 Poppy Appeal, an organisation which funds support services for New Zealand's veterans, former and current servicemen and -women and their dependents. It is available digitally.

Sadly, Jim died at the age of 103 on 2 October 2022, three years to the day on which he was inducted into the New Zealand Music Hall of Fame.[3] He was recognised along with Ruru Karaitiana and Pixie Williams to celebrate the seventieth anniversary of 'Blue Smoke'.

'Find Your Way Back' (Neil Finn, featuring Stevie Nicks and Christine McVie)

Written by Neil Finn
Duration: 3:17
Released as a single in May 2020 (Lester Records)

A potential insight into how a Neil Finn and Fleetwood Mac collaboration would have sounded if they'd recorded an album. The sad passing of Christine McVie seems to have put paid to any future activity from the band. The song features Fleetwood Mac's Stevie Nicks, Christine McVie and Mike Campbell, along with Elroy Finn and fellow Kiwi singer Georgia Nott. It was a digital release during COVID with the proceeds going to Homeground, a project developed by the Auckland City Mission.

The song is a beautiful, shimmering number that incorporates the vocal talents of Neil Finn and Stevie Nicks excellently. The slide guitars glide in and out of the arrangement to give the song that reflective and ethereal charm. The backing vocals add to the atmospheric nature of the song.

'Better Times Will Come' (Janis Ian with Neil Finn)

Written by Janis Ian
Duration: 2:27
Released in May 2020

One of the positive experiences of appearing on the BBC's *Songwriter's Circle* in 2011 was Neil's collaboration with Janis Ian, the American singer-songwriter. The nature of the series was to invite some performers each week to play their songs; they were accompanied by the other two guests from that episode. Ryan Adams was the other performer on the show, who was less than gracious in accepting the show's requirements. The less said about Adams here, the one plus was that the show led to this collaboration.

Janis Ian talks up the story of how the song came together:

> I invited Neil to this project, and he politely responded that his hands were full with finishing up a new album, writing projects and babysitting grandchildren. So, imagine my surprise when an MP3 arrived out of the blue with a note from Neil saying, 'It's a lovely intimate performance from you, so I just played along with your recording and tried to make it feel like we were in the same room. Hope you like it.' As though I wouldn't....[4]

Janis takes the lead on this one with Neil Finn's guitar and harmonies seamlessly added to the mix. It is a delicate and emotional number. The title fits in with the feeling that everyone around the world was hoping for at the time of the release. It is a beautifully simple but effective song.

'Artist in Residence' (Todd Rundgren featuring Neil Finn)

Written by Todd Rundgren and Neil Finn
Duration: 3:13
Released on Todd Rundgren's *Space Force* album in October 2022

This collaboration took a long time to release, given that it is from an album featuring other guest performers. Then add in a global pandemic and it would not be until 2023 that it finally came out.

The song features Neil Finn on vocals, in a style that would not sound out of place on one of his solo releases. It features a heavily treated electronic bed. The vocals from Neil Finn feature the falsetto that he has employed successfully on some of his latter-day songs.

'Here Comes the Season Again'

Written by Gregg Turkington and Erik Paparozzi
Duration: 3:13
Released on the *Neil Hamburger Presents Seasonal Depression Suite* album in November 2023

This is a collaboration from Neil Hamburger's satirical album *Seasonal Depression Suite*. The song is a tongue-in-cheek Christmas song, asking why there are no new seasonal songs for the kids. They may have inadvertently written a new Christmas standard here.

It is a straightforward piano ballad with the descending chords adding to the down-tempo feel. If you are averse to upbeat, clichéd Christmas songs, this may be the song for you.

Appendix

Crowded House Discography

Studio Albums

Crowded House (July 1986) (Capitol)
Temple Of Low Men (July 1988) (Capitol)
Woodface (July 1991) (Capitol)
Together Alone (October 1993) (Capitol)
Time On Earth (June 2007) (Parlophone/ EMI)
Intriguer (June 2010) (Fantasy/Universal)
Dreamers Are Waiting (June 2021) (EMI/Lester Records)
Gravity Stairs (May 2024) (BMG/Lester Records)

Compilations

Recurring Dream: The Very Best of Crowded House (June 1996) (Capitol)
Afterglow (December 1999) (Capitol)
*Classic Masters** (June 2003) (EMI/Capitol)
The Very, Very Best of Crowded House (October 2010) (Capitol/EMI)
*US-only compilation.

There are other compilations, including *The Essential (2003/2011), Platinum Crowded House* (2007) and *All the Best/Gold (2012)*. These have all been issued by EMI/Capitol/Universal. They are cheap, low-thrills (the artwork/liner notes, not the music) compilations.

Singles

'Mean to Me' (1986)

'World Where You Live' (1986)
'Now We're Getting Somewhere' (1986)
'Don't Dream It's Over' (1986)
'Something So Strong' (1987)
'Better Be Home Soon Temple of Low Men' (1988)
'When You Come'(1988)
'Into Temptation' (1988)
'Never Be the Same'(1988)
'Sister Madly' (1989)
'I Feel Possessed' (1990)
'Chocolate Cake' (1991)
'Fall at Your Feet' (1991)
'It's Only Natural' (1991)
'Weather with You' (1992)
'Four Seasons in One Day' (1992)
'Distant Sun' (1993)
'Nails in My Feet' (1994)
'Locked Out'(1994)
'Fingers of Love'(1994)
'Pineapple Head' (1994)
'Private Universe' (1995)
'Together Alone'(1995)
'Everything Is Good for You' (1996)
'Instinct'(1996)
'Not the Girl You Think You Are'(1996)
'Don't Dream It's Over' (UK re-release) (1996)
'Don't Stop Now' (2007)
'She Called Up' (2007)
'Pour Le Monde'(2007)
'Saturday Sun' (2007)
'Either Side of the World' (2007)
'Whatever You Want' (2020)
'To the Island' (2020)
'Playing With Fire' (2021)
'Oh Hi' (2024)
'Teenage Summer' (2024)
'The Howl' (2024)

Neil Finn

Studio Albums

Try Whistling This (June 1998) (Parlophone)

One Nil (March 2001) (Parlophone)
One All (2002) (North American release of *One Nil*) (Nettwerk America)
Dizzy Heights (February 2014) (Lester, Kobalt)
Out of Silence (September 2017) (Lester)
Solo at the Seymour Centre, 2010 (October 2019) (Black Box Records)
Neil Finn: Sessions At West 54th (April 2025 (Sony BMG) (Legacy Recordings)

Singles

'Sinner' (1998)
'She Will Have Her Way' (1998)
'Last One Standing'(1999)
'Rest of the Day Off' (2001)
'Wherever You Are' (2001)
'Last to Know'(2001)
'Hole in the Ice' (2001)
'Driving Me Mad' (2002)
'Dizzy Heights'(2014)
'Flying in the Face of Love' (2014)
'More Than One of You' (2017)
'Second Nature'(2017)
'Find Your Way Back Home' (with Stevie Nicks and Christine McVie) (2020)

7 Worlds Collide

Albums

7 Worlds Collide (February 2002) (Parlophone)
The Sun Came Out (August 2009) (Sony)

The Finn Brothers

Albums

Finn (1995)
Everyone is Here (2004)

Singles

'Suffer Never'(1994)
'Angel's Heap' (1994)
'Won't Give In' (2004)

'Nothing Wrong with You' (2005)
'Anything Can Happen' (2005)
'Part of Me, Part of You' (2005)

Neil Finn and Paul Kelly

Goin' Your Way (November 2013) (EMI)

Neil Finn and Liam Finn

Lightsleeper (August 2018) (Inertia/PIAS)

Split Enz

Studio Albums

Mental Notes (1975)
Second Thoughts (The second album, albeit released in Europe with tracks from *Mental Notes*) (1976)
Dizrythmia (1977)*
Frenzy (1979)**
The Beginning of the Enz (1979, recorded 1973–1974)
True Colours (1980)
Waiata (titled *Corroboree* in Australia) (1981)
Time and Tide (1982)
Conflicting Emotions (1983)
See Ya 'Round (1984)
*The album on which Neil Finn joined as a member of Split Enz.
** Neil Finn's first contributions as a songwriter appear on the original 1979 release, co-writing 'Give It a Whirl' and 'Mind Over Matter'.

Endnotes

Acknowledgements

1. B. Drummond, 'Sixty', Caught By the River, 13 May 2013, www.caughtbytheriver.net/2013/05/sixty-bill-drummond/, accessed 20 April 2025.
2. P. Paphides, 'Don't Stream It's Over', *Record Collector Magazine,* July 2024.

Introduction

1. H. Hirway, 'Crowded House—Don't Dream It's Over'. Episode 274, Song Exploder. www.songexploder.net/crowded-house, accessed 20 April 2025.
2. C. Harvey, *Make Music with Crowded House* (UK: International Music Publishers, 2002).

1. *Crowded House* (1986)

1. C. Bourke, *Something So Strong* (Australia: Pan Macmillan, 1997).
2. Ibid.
3. Ibid.
4. C. Harvey, *Make Music with Crowded House.*
5. C. Bourke, *Something So Strong.*
6. Crowded House (2016 Deluxe Edition CD, Sleeve Notes) (Universal/Capitol).
7. www.neilfinn.com/mean-to-me, accessed 3 January 2025.
8. www.neilfinn.com/crowded-house-deluxe-edition, accessed 17 January 2025.
9. www.neilfinn.com/now-were-getting-somewhere, accessed 17 January 2025.

10. H. Hirway, 'Crowded House—Don't Dream It's Over'. Song Exploder.
11. www.neilfinn.com/dont-dream-its-over, accessed 12 January 2025.
12. C. Bourke, *Something So Strong.*
13 C. Bourke, *Something So Strong.*
14. H. Hirway, *Crowded House—Don't Dream It's Over.*
15. www.neilfinn.com/love-you-til-the-day-i-die, accessed 3 January 2025.
16. www.neilfinn.com/something-so-strong, accessed 3 January 2025.
17. www.neilfinn.com/thats-what-i-call-love, accessed 3 January 2025.

2. *Temple of Low Men* (1988)

1. C. Bourke, *Something So Strong.*
2. R. Christgau, '*Christgau's Consumer Guide*'. (Village Voice, 1988). www.robertchristgau.com/xg/cg/cgvts88-88.php, accessed 18 June 2025.
3. Temple of Low Men (2016 Deluxe Edition CD, Sleeve Notes) (Universal/Capitol).
4. www.neilfinn.com/kill-eye, accessed 12 December 2024.
5. www.neilfinn.com/into-temptation, accessed 12 December 2024.
6. www.neilfinn.com/mansion-in-the-slums, accessed 12 December 2024.
7. www.neilfinn.com/when-you-come, accessed 12 December 2024.
8. www.neilfinn.com/never-be-the-same, accessed 12 December 2024.
9. www.neilfinn.com/love-this-life, accessed 12 December 2024.
10. www.neilfinn.com/in-the-lowlands, accessed 12 December 2024.
11. www.neilfinn.com/better-be-home-soon, accessed 12 December 2024.
12. *Neil Finn: The Legacy of Crowded House and Their Greatest Hits | Essentials* (2021). www.youtube.com/watch?v=YoxoFEhl-t4, accessed 16 May 2025.

3. *Woodface* (1991)

1. G. Thomson, 'Crowded House'. *The Word.* Rock's Backpages. www.rocksbackpages.com/Library/Article/crowded-house, accessed 8 July 2025.
2. *Woodface* (2016 Deluxe Edition CD, Sleeve Notes) (Universal/Capitol).
3. J. Apter, *Don't Dream It's Over: The Remarkable Life of Neil Finn.*
4. *Enough Rope with Andrew Denton*, web.archive.org/web/20110817105338/http://www.abc.net.au/tv/enoughrope/transcripts/s1979899.htm, accessed 17 August 2025.
5. J. Apter, *Don't Dream It's Over: The Remarkable Life of Neil Finn.*
6. Ibid.
7. www.neilfinn.com/its-only-natural, accessed 22 December 2024.
8. G. Thomson, *Crowded House.*
9. J. Apter, *Don't Dream It's Over: The Remarkable Life of Neil Finn.*

10. G. Thomson, *Crowded House.*
11. *Crowded House: Woodface - Great Australian Albums* (2007) www.youtube.com/watch?v=blPfoGJi-LU.
12. J. Apter, *Don't Dream It's Over: The Remarkable Life of Neil Finn.*
13. *Crowded House Woodface Great Australian Albums* (2007) www.youtube.com/watch?v=blPfoGJi-LU, accessed 6 June 2025.
14. *Woodface* (2016 Deluxe Edition CD, Sleeve Notes) (Universal/Capitol)
15. www.neilfinn.com/chocolate-cake, accessed 22 December 2024.
16. J. Apter, *Don't Dream It's Over: The Remarkable Life of Neil Finn.*
17. *Crowded House Woodface Great Australian Albums.*
18. www.neilfinn.com/fall-at-your-feet, accessed 22 December 2024.
19. www.neilfinn.com/fall-at-your-feet, accessed 22 December 2024.
20. J. Azlewood, (2024), *Neil Finn Interviewed: 'I took acid and slept in John and Yoko's bed.'* www.mojo4music.com/articles/stories/neil-finn-interviewed/, accessed 6 January 2025.
21. www.neilfinn.com/weather-with-you, accessed 12 December 2024.
22. www.neilfinn.com/weather-with-you, accessed 12 December 2024.
23. www.neilfinn.com/whispers-and-moans, accessed 12 December 2024.
24. www.neilfinn.com/four-seasons-in-one-day, accessed 12 December 2024.
25. www.neilfinn.com/four-seasons-in-one-day, accessed 12 December 2024.
26. www.neilfinn.com/there-goes-god, accessed 12 December 2024.
27. www.neilfinn.com/fame-is, accessed 12 December 2024.
28. www.neilfinn.com/all-i-ask, accessed 12 December 2024.
29. www.neilfinn.com/as-sure-as-i-am, accessed 12 December 2024.
30. www.neilfinn.com/italian-plastic, accessed 20 December 2024.
31. www.neilfinn.com/italian-plastic, accessed 20 December 2024.
32. www.neilfinn.com/she-goes-on, accessed 20 December 2024.
33. www.neilfinn.com/how-will-you-go, accessed 20 December 2024.
34. C. Bourke, *Something So Strong.*
35. www.neilfinn.com/how-will-you-go, accessed 20 December 2024.

4. *Together Alone* (1993)

1. www.neilfinn.com/kare-kare, accessed 27 December 2024.
2. J. Apter, *Don't Dream It's Over: The Remarkable Life of Neil Finn.*
3. *Together Alone* (2016 Deluxe Edition CD, Sleeve Notes) (Universal/Capitol).
4. S. Maconie, (1994) *'Crowded House: The Fine Art of Surfacing'*. Q. www.rocksbackpages.com/Library/Article/crowded-house-the-fine-art-of-surfacing.
5. P. Sutcliffe, (1993) *Crowded House: Crowded House OBE.* Q. Rock's Backpages. www.rocksbackpages.com/Library/Article/crowded-house-crowded-house-obe, accessed 6 January 2025.
6. S. Maconie, *Crowded House: The Fine Art of Surfacing.*
7. Ibid.

8. Ibid.
9. J. Apter, *Don't Dream It's Over: The Remarkable Life of Neil Finn.*
10. *Together Alone* (2016 Deluxe Edition CD, Sleeve Notes) (Universal/Capitol).
11. Ibid.
12. www.neilfinn.com/kare-kare, accessed 4 May 2025.
13. S. Maconie, *Crowded House: The Fine Art of Surfacing.*
14. www.neilfinn.com/fingers-of-love, accessed 4 May 2025.
15. www.neilfinn.com/locked-out, accessed 4 May 2025.
16. www.neilfinn.com/pineapple-head, accessed 4 May 2025.
17. www.neilfinn.com/private-universe, accessed 4 May 2025.
18. www.neilfinn.com/distant-sun, accessed 4 May 2025.
19. www.neilfinn.com/together-alone-1, accessed 4 May 2025.

5. *Recurring Dream: The Very Best of Crowded House* (1996)

1. C. Bourke, *Something So Strong.*
2. www.neilfinn.com/recurring-dream, accessed 4 May 2025.
3. www.neilfinn.com/not-the-girl-you-think-you-are, accessed 14 May 2025.
4. www.neilfinn.com/instinct, accessed 14 May 2025.

6. *Afterglow* (1999)

1. Fangradio: Wednesday 6 May 2020, www.fangradio.com, accessed 4 June 2025.
2. *Afterglow* (2016 Deluxe Edition CD, Sleeve Notes) (Universal/Capitol).
3. www.neilfinn.com/i-am-in-love, accessed 6 June 2025.
4. www.neilfinn.com/i-am-in-love, accessed 6 June 2025.
5. www.neilfinn.com/sacred-cow, accessed 6 June 2025.
6. www.neilfinn.com/you-can-touch, accessed 6 June 2025.
7. www.neilfinn.com/the-diary-2015/2015/9/11/crowded-house-help-is-coming, accessed 8 June 2025.
8. www.neilfinn.com/help-is-coming, accessed 8 June 2025.
9. www.neilfinn.com/i-love-you-dawn, accessed 8 June 2025.
10. www.neilfinn.com/dr-livingstone, accessed 8 June 2025.
11. www.neilfinn.com/my-tellys-gone-bung, accessed 8 June 2025.
12. www.neilfinn.com/lester, accessed 8 June 2025.
13. www.neilfinn.com/anyone-can-tell, accessed 8 June 2025.
14. www.neilfinn.com/recurring-dream-lyrics, accessed 8 June 2025.
15. www.neilfinn.com/left-hand, accessed 8 June 2025.
16. www.neilfinn.com/time-immemorial, accessed 8 June 2025.
17. www.neilfinn.com/spirit-of-the-stairs, accessed 8 June 2025.
18. www.neilfinn.com/im-so-scared-of-losing-i-cant-compete, accessed 10 June 2025.
19. www.neilfinn.com/taste-of-something-divine, accessed 10 June 2025.
20. *Afterglow* (2016 Deluxe Edition CD, Sleeve Notes) (Universal/Capitol)

7. *Time on Earth* (2007)

1. Enough Rope with Andrew Denton.
2. www.neilfinn.com/time-on-earth, accessed 10 June 2025.
3. www.neilfinn.com/time-on-earth, accessed 10 June 2025.
4. *Time on Earth* (2016 Deluxe Edition CD, Sleeve Notes) (Universal/Capitol).
5. www.neilfinn.com/nobody-wants-to, accessed 14 June 2025.
6. www.neilfinn.com/dont-stop-now, accessed 14 June 2025.
7. *Time on Earth* (2016 Deluxe Edition CD, Sleeve Notes) (Universal/Capitol).
8. www.neilfinn.com/say-that-again, accessed 14 June 2025.
9. www.neilfinn.com/pour-le-monde, accessed 14 June 2025.
10. www.neilfinn.com/even-a-child, accessed 14 June.
11. www.neilfinn.com/a-sigh, accessed 14 June 2025.
12. www.neilfinn.com/silent-house, accessed 14 June 2025.
13. www.neilfinn.com/silent-house, accessed 14 June 2025.
14. www.neilfinn.com/silent-house, accessed 14 June 2025.
15. www.neilfinn.com/english-trees, accessed 14 June 2025.
16. www.neilfinn.com/english-trees, accessed 24 June 2025.
17. www.neilfinn.com/walked-her-way-down, accessed 14 June 2025.
18. www.neilfinn.com/transit-lounge, accessed 24 June 2025.
19. www.neilfinn.com/you-are-the-one-to-make-me-cry, accessed 24 June 2025.
20. www.neilfinn.com/people-are-like-suns, accessed 24 June 2025.
21. www.neilfinn.com/heres-a-note, accessed 24 June 2025.
22. www.neilfinn.com/purple-light, accessed 24 June 2025.
23. *Time on Earth* (2016 Deluxe Edition CD, Sleeve Notes) (Universal/Capitol).
24. www.neilfinn.com/stare-me-out, accessed 24 June 2025.
25. *Time on Earth* (2016 Deluxe Edition CD, Sleeve Notes) (Universal/Capitol).
26. Crowded House - Album By Album: Time On Earth, 25 February 2021 www.fangradio.com, accessed 25 June 2025.
27. www.neilfinn.com/bound-to-rescue, accessed 24 June 2025.
28. *Time on Earth (2016 Deluxe Edition CD, Sleeve Notes) (Universal/Capitol).*

8. *Intriguer* (2010)

1. *Crowded House Intriguer Insider*: www.youtube.com/watch?v=9cxsufCh_9g, accessed 7 June 2025.
2. www.neilfinn.com/intriguer, accessed 27 June 2025.
3. *Intriguer* (2016 Deluxe Edition CD, Sleeve Notes) (Universal/Capitol).
4. www.neilfinn.com/saturday-sun, accessed 27 June 2025.
5. www.neilfinn.com/archers-arrows, accessed 27 June 2025.

6. www.neilfinn.com/falling-dove, accessed 27 June 2025.
7. www.neilfinn.com/isolation, accessed 27 June 2025.
8. *Intriguer* (2016 Deluxe Edition CD, Sleeve Notes) (Universal/Capitol).
9. www.neilfinn.com/twice-if-youre-lucky, accessed 27 June 2025.
10. www.neilfinn.com/even-if, accessed 27 June 2025.
11. www.neilfinn.com/only-way-to-go-is-forwards, accessed 27 June 2025.
12. www.neilfinn.com/god-lives-over-the-road, accessed 28 June 2025.
13. www.neilfinn.com/turn-it-around, accessed 28 June 2025.
14. www.neilfinn.com/two-minutes-of-silence, accessed 28 June 2025.
15. www.neilfinn.com/two-minutes-of-silence, accessed 28 June 2025.
16. www.neilfinn.com/nonsense-of-course, accessed 28 June 2025.
17. www.neilfinn.com/strangest-friends, accessed 28 June 2025.

10. *The Very, Very Best of Crowded House* (2010)

1. neilfinn.com/strangest-friends, accessed 28 June 2025.

11. *Dreamers Are Waiting* (2021)

1. J. Apter, *Don't Dream It's Over: The Remarkable Life of Neil Finn.*
2. C. Schulz, (2021). Inside Crowded House's comeback: 'This is actually delusional.' www.stuff.co.nz/entertainment/music/300238618/inside-crowded-houses-comeback-this-is-actually-delusional, accessed 3 February 2025.
3. P. Kirkley, (2024) '*Defying Gravity*'. Classic Pop Magazine (May/June 2024).
4. C. Schulz, (2021). Inside Crowded House's comeback: 'This is actually delusional'.
5. www.neilfinn.com/to-the-island-lyrics, accessed 8 July 2025.
6. www.neilfinn.com/to-the-island-lyrics, accessed 8 July 2025.
7. Crowded House, *'To the Island'*, www.youtube.com/watch?v=-HGjvQxGxNQ
8. www.neilfinn.com/sweet-tooth, accessed 8 July 2025.
9. Crowded House, '*Sweet Tooth*', www.youtube.com/watch?v=QMJOyW_sEGQ, accessed 9 April 2025.
10. Crowded House '*Whatever You Want*' www.youtube.com/watch?v=ZggTaHMoQYs, accessed 9 April 2025.
11. J. Bruce, (2020) '*Crowded House release 'Whatever You Want', their first song in a decade, with video starring Mac DeMarco*'. www.nme.com/news/music/crowded-house-team-up-with-mac-demarco-for-whatever-you-want-their-first-song-in-a-decade-2802826, accessed 29 April 2025.
12. P. Sinclair, (2021). *Crowded House / Dreamers Are Waiting: Track-by-track*. www.superdeluxeedition.com/reviews/crowded-house-dreamers-are-waiting-track-by-track/, accessed 3 March 2025.
13. Ibid.
14. P. Paphides, (2024) 'Don't Stream It's Over'. *Record Collector Magazine.*

15. www.neilfinn.com/too-good-for-this-world, accessed 14 July 2025.
16. www.crowdedhouse.com/post/love-isnt-hard-at-all, accessed 14 July 2025.

12. *Gravity Stairs* (2024)

1. P. Sinclair, (2021). *Neil Finn and Mitchell Froom of Crowded House in conversation with SDE*. www.superdeluxeedition.com/interview/neil-finn-and-mitchell-froom-of-crowded-house-in-conversation-with-sde/, accessed 4 April 2025.
2. P. Kirkley, (2024) 'Defying Gravity'. *Classic Pop Magazine* (May/June 2024).
3. J. Jennings, *Crowded House: House Is Where the Heart Is*. www.au.rollingstone.com/music/music-features/crowded-house-rolling-stone-cover-story-62030, accessed 16 April 2025.
4. Ibid.
5. A. Zaleski, (2024) *We've Got A File On You: Neil Finn*. www.stereogum.com/2265812/weve-got-a-file-on-you-neil-finn/interviews/weve-got-a-file-on-you/, accessed 5 February 2025.
6. *Kyle Meredith with... Neil Finn* (Crowded House) https://www.youtube.com/watch?v=CTfOge8-wsY, accessed 7 May 2025.
7. G. Paul, (2024) *Crowded House Talks Touring, Latest Album 'Gravity Stairs,' and Family Ties* (The Interview) www.rockcellarmagazine.com/crowded-house-interview-neil-finn-gravity-stairs-tour-dates/, accessed 14 July 2025.
8. RNZ: Neil Finn: Live in studio with new Crowded House album. www.rnz.co.nz/national/programmes/music101/audio/2018940931/neil-finn-live-in-studio-with-new-crowded-house-album, accessed 16 May 2025.
9. www.crowdedhouse.com/post/cavern-club, accessed 24 July 2025.
10. Z. Lowe. *Neil Finn: Crowded House, Gravity Stairs, & Influence of The Beatles | Apple Music*: www.youtube.com/watch?v=hgXarIof-So, accessed June 2025
11. G. Paul, *Crowded House Talks Touring, Latest Album 'Gravity Stairs,' and Family Ties.*
12. www.neilfinn.com/magic-piano-lyrics, accessed 21 July 2025.
13. P. Kirkley, (2024), 'Defying Gravity', *Classic Pop Magazine* (May/June 2024).
14. Ibid.
15. www.neilfinn.com/magic-piano-lyrics, accessed 21 July 2025.
16. www.neilfinn.com/teenage-summer, accessed 21 July 2025.
17. A. Zaleski, (2024) '*We've Got A File On You: Neil Finn*'.
18. J. Jennings, '*Crowded House: House Is Where the Heart Is*'.
19. www.neilfinn.com/teenage-summer, accessed 21 July 2025.
20. *Crowded House - Teenage Summer: Behind The Music*: www.youtube.com/watch?v=Kbc4xkzsEfE, accessed 5 May 2025.

21. Z. Lowe. *Neil Finn: Crowded House, Gravity Stairs, & Influence of The Beatles.*
22. Crowded House - *Teenage Summer* (Official Music Video): www.youtube.be/DDXlz2srXOg, accessed 14 July 2025.
23. Crowded House - *The Howl: Behind the Music*: www.youtube.com/watch?v=3k0XwlPnE0g, accessed 15 July 2025.
24. Crowded House - *The Howl* (Official Music Video): www.youtube.com/watch?v=MFln0Ll2s6A accessed 15 July 2025.
25. www.neilfinn.com/all-that-i-can-ever-own, accessed 21 July 2025.
26. Crowded House - *Oh Hi (Official Music Video*): www.youtube.com/watch?v=_uMmTV4oGaA, accessed 14 June 2025.
27. Crowded House: *Oh Hi x So They Can* (Official Charity Video): www.youtube.com/watch?v=JU8ZXkx0c3E&t=27s, accessed 14 June 2025.
28. *Kyle Meredith with... Neil Finn* (Crowded House).
29. A. Zaleski, *We've Got A File On You: Neil Finn.*
30. www.neilfinn.com/journal/2024/10/3/some-greater-plan
31. *Neil Finn: Crowded House, Gravity Stairs, & Influence of The Beatles.*
32. *Crowded House - Some Greater Plan (For Claire*) (Official Music Video): www.youtube.com/watch?v=G0pRUAbteDU, accessed 7 July 2025.
33. *Neil Finn: Crowded House, Gravity Stairs, & Influence of The Beatles.*
34. Ibid.
35. A. Zaleski, We've Got A File On You: Neil Finn.
36. G. Graf, '*The guitar allows me to switch my brain off from trying to understand the music... The mistakes make it interesting. Crowded House's Neil Finn on his trial-and-error approach to playing and songwriting*': www.guitarplayer.com/players/the-guitar-allows-me-to-switch-my-brain-off-from-trying-to-understand-the-music-the-mistakes-make-it-interesting-crowded-houses-neil-finn-on-his-trial-and-error-approach-to-playing-and-songwriting, accessed 1 July 2025.
37. G. Paul, *Crowded House Talks Touring, Latest Album 'Gravity Stairs,' and Family Ties.*
38. *Kyle Meredith with... Neil Finn* (Crowded House).
39. www.neilfinn.com/crowded-house-gravity-stairs, accessed 23 July 2025.
40. www.neilfinn.com/crowded-house-gravity-stairs, accessed 23 July 2025.

13. Neil Finn: The Solo Years (1994–2025)

1. G. Reid, *Recommended Record: The Finn Brothers, Finn (Lester):* www.elsewhere.co.nz/music/10387/recommended-record-the-finn-brothers-finn-lester/, accessed 15 February 2025.
2. L. Gava, *Classic Album Revisited: Neil Finn – 'Try Whistling This'* www.xsnoize.com/classic-album-revisited-neil-finn-try-whistling-this/, accessed 19 May 2025.

3. www.neilfinn.com/one-nil, accessed 27 July 2025.
4. www.neilfinn.com/dont-ask-why, accessed 27 July 2025.
5. www.neilfinn.com/rain, accessed 27 July 2025.
6. E. Green, www.thelogbook.com/music/neil-finn-rain/, accessed 1 March 2025.
7. A. Zaleski, (2024). *We've Got a File On You: Neil Finn.*
8. www.neilfinn.com/one-all, accessed 27 July 2025.
9. www.neilfinn.com/everyone-is-here, accessed 27 July 2025.
10. www.neilfinn.com/edible-flowers, accessed 27 July 2025.
11. J. Scherer, *Rocky ride for Wilco*: https://www.stuff.co.nz/entertainment/3600250/Rocky-ride-for-Wilco, accessed 17 April 2025.
12. Neil Finn & Paul Kelly—Goin' Your way 2013. (EMI/Omnivore CD Sleeve Notes)
13. Ibid
14. S. King. www.goodreads.com/quotes/615980-write-with-the-door-closed-rewrite-with-the-door-open, accessed 16 July 2025.
15. P. Sinclair, *Neil Finn to record new studio album 'live on the internet'* https://superdeluxeedition.com/news/neil-finn-to-record-new-studio-album-live-on-the-internet/, accessed 1 May 2025.
16. www.neilfinn.com/out-of-silence, accessed 7 July 2025.
17. www.neilfinn.com/lightsleeper, accessed 7 July 2025.
18. www.neilfinn.com/lightsleeper, accessed 7 July 2025.
19. www.neilfinn.com/lightsleeper, accessed 7 July 2025.
20. www.neilfinn.com/journal/2020/10/3/solo-at-the-seymour-centre-2010, accessed 7 July 2025.

14. Selected Solo Tracks

1. www.neilfinn.com/song-of-the-lonely-mountain, accessed 27 July 2025.
2. *Neil Finn with Jim Carter - Blue Smoke (Anzac Day/2015) - Extended video* www.youtube.com/watch?v=5leUxBMsrbY, accessed 7 April 2025.
3. *NZ Music Hall of Fame Inductees—Ruru Karaitiana, Pixie Williams, Jim Carter*. www.undertheradar.co.nz/news/16264/NZ-Music-Hall-Of-Fame-Inductees--Ruru-Karaitiana-Pixie-Williams-Jim- Carter.utr, accessed 3 April 2025.
4. The 'Better Times' Project Janis Ian & Friends: www.bettertimeswillcome.com/song_page/neil-finn/, accessed 3 March 2025.

Bibliography

Books

Apter, J. *Don't Dream It's Over: The Remarkable Life of Neil Finn* (UK: Jawbone, 2024)

Bourke, C. *Something So Strong* (Australia: Pan Macmillan, 1997)

Harvey, C. *Make Music with Crowded House* (UK: International Music Publishers, 2002)

Documentaries and Interviews

Crowded House: Woodface, Great Australian Albums (2007) www.youtube.com/watch?v=blPfoGJi-LU

Crowded House, *Teenage Summer: Behind The Music*, www.youtube.com/watch?v=Kbc4xkzsEfE bn

Neil Finn: The Legacy of Crowded House and Their Greatest Hits | Essentials (2021). www.youtube.com/watch?v=YoxoFEhl-t4

Neil Finn with Jim Carter, *Blue Smoke (Anzac Day/2015)*, Extended video www.youtube.com/watch?v=5leUxBMsrbY

RNZ: Neil Finn: Live in studio with new Crowded House album, www.rnz.co.nz/national/programmes/music101/audio/2018940931/neil-finn-live-in-studio-with-new-crowded-house-album

Kyle Meredith with... Neil Finn (Crowded House), www.youtube.com/watch?v=CTfOge8-wsY

Lowe, Z., *Neil Finn: Crowded House, Gravity Stairs, & Influence of The Beatles*, Apple Music: www.youtube.com/watch?v=hgXarIof-So

Music Videos

'Sweet Tooth' Video: www.youtube.com/watch?v=QMJOyW_sEGQ
'To the Island': www.youtube.com/watch?v=-HGjvQxGxNQ
'Whatever You Want': www.youtube.com/watch?v=ZggTaHMoQYs
'Some Greater Plan' (A Song for Clare): www.youtube.com/watch?v=G0pRUAbteDU

Newspapers and Magazines

Azlewood, J., Neil Finn interviewed: 'I took acid and slept in John and Yoko's bed.' *Mojo*.
www.mojo4music.com/articles/stories/neil-finn-interviewed/ 2024

Bourke, C., 'My Second Life Has Just Begun'. Book Excerpt. Crowded House. *Rock's Backpages*. www.rocksbackpages.com/Library/Article/my-second-life-has-just-begun--april-1994

Brandle, L., Neil Finn Talks 'Master' Kevin Parker, Touring Post-COVID and New Crowded House Album *Dreamers Are Waiting*, *Billboard* 2021 https://www.billboard.com/music/music-news/neil-finn-kevin-parker-interview-crowded-house-dreamers-are-waiting-9581210/

Bruce, J., Crowded House release 'Whatever You Want', their first song in a decade, with video starring Mac DeMarco, *NME*, 2024, www.nme.com/news/music/crowded-house-team-up-with-mac-demarco-for-whatever-you-want-their-first-song-in-a-decade-2802826

Christgau, R., *Christgau's Consumer Guide*, Village Voice, 1988, www.robertchristgau.com/xg/cg/cgvts88-88.php

Drummond, B., Sixty, *Caught By the River*, 13 May 2013, www.caughtbytheriver.net/2013/05/sixty-bill-drummond/

Graff, G., The guitar allows me to switch my brain off from trying to understand the music... The mistakes make it interesting. Crowded House's Neil Finn on his trial-and-error approach to playing and songwriting: www.guitarplayer.com/players/the-guitar-allows-me-to-switch-my-brain-off-from-trying-to-understand-the-music-the-mistakes-make-it-interesting-crowded-houses-neil-finn-on-his-trial-and-error-approach-to-playing-and-songwriting, Guitar Player, 2024.

Jennings, J. (2024) 'Crowded House: House Is Where the Heart Is.' *Rolling Stone*. www.au.rollingstone.com/music/music-features/crowded-house-rolling-stone-cover-story-62030

Kirkley, P. 'Defying Gravity'. *Classic Pop Magazine*, May/June 2024.

Green, E., Rain, *The Logbook*, 2022. www.thelogbook.com/music/neil-finn-rain/

Paul, G. (2024) Crowded House Talks Touring, Latest Album 'Gravity Stairs,' and Family Ties (The Interview) www.rockcellarmagazine.com/crowded-house-interview-neil-finn-gravity-stairs-tour-dates/

MOJO., Crowded House Interviewed: 'I definitely take responsibility for making some quite poor decisions in the band's career', MOJO, 2024. www.mojo4music.com/articles/stories/crowded-house-interviewed/

Paphides, P. (2024) 'Don't Stream It's Over'. Record Collector Magazine.

Schulz, C., Inside Crowded House's comeback: 'This is actually delusional', *Stuff*, 2021.

www.stuff.co.nz/entertainment/music/300238618/inside-crowded-houses-comeback-this-is-actually-delusional

Sinclair, P., Neil Finn to record new studio album 'live on the internet', *SDE*, 2021

www.superdeluxeedition.com/news/neil-finn-to-record-new-studio-album-live-on-the-internet/

Sinclair, P., Crowded House / Dreamers Are Waiting: Track-by-track. SDE, 2021.

www.superdeluxeedition.com/reviews/crowded-house-dreamers-are-waiting-track-by-track/

Sinclair, P., Neil Finn and Mitchell Froom of Crowded House in conversation with SDE. SDE, 2021 www.superdeluxeedition.com/interview/neil-finn-and-mitchell-froom-of-crowded-house-in-conversation-with-sde/

Sutcliffe, P., Crowded House: Crowded House OBE, *Q*, 1993, Rock's Backpages, www.rocksbackpages.com/Library/Article/crowded-house-crowded-house-obe

Thomson, G., Crowded House. *The Word*, 2011, Rock's Backpages. www.rocksbackpages.com/Library/Article/crowded-house

Under the Radar., NZ Music Hall of Fame Inductees—Ruru Karaitiana, Pixie Williams, Jim Carter, 2019, www.undertheradar.co.nz/news/16264/NZ-Music-Hall-Of-Fame-Inductees--Ruru-Karaitiana-Pixie-Williams-Jim-Carter.utr

Zaleski, A., We've Got A File On You: Neil Finn, 2024, Stereogum. www.stereogum.com/2265812/weve-got-a-file-on-you-neil-finn/interviews/weve-got-a-file-on-you/

Podcasts

Denton, A., Neil Finn and Nick Seymour *Enough Rope with Andrew Denton*, 16 July 2007 www.web.archive.org/web/20110817105338/http://www.abc.net.au/tv/enoughrope/transcripts/s1979899.htm

Hirway, H., Crowded House—Don't Dream It's Over Episode 274, Song Exploder. June 2024, www.songexploder.net/crowded-house

Neil Finn: The Legacy of Crowded House and Their Greatest Hits | Essentials (2021).

www.youtube.com/watch?v=YoxoFEhl-t4

Setlists Crowded House Set Lists

www.setlist.fm/setlists/crowded-house-6bd6ae3a.html

Sleeve Notes/Recordings

Crowded House

Crowded House (2016 Deluxe Edition) (Universal/Capitol)
Temple of Low Men (2016 Deluxe Edition) (Universal/Capitol)
Woodface (2016 Deluxe Edition) (Universal/Capitol)
Together Alone (2016 Deluxe Edition) (Universal/Capitol)
Recurring Dream (2016 Deluxe Edition) (Universal/Capitol)
Afterglow (2016 Deluxe Edition) (Universal/Capitol)
Time on Earth (2016 Deluxe Edition) (Universal/Capitol)
Intriguer (2016 Deluxe Edition) (Universal/Capitol)
Out of Silence (2017) (Lester Records)
Dreamers Are Waiting (2021) (Lester Records)
Gravity Stairs (2024) (Lester Records)

The Finn Brothers

Finn (1995) (Parlophone/EMI)
Everyone is Here (2004) (Nettwerk/ Parlophone)

Neil Finn

Try Whistling This (1998) (Parlophone)
One Nil (2001) (Parlophone)
One All (2002) (Nettwerk America)
Dizzy Heights (2014) (Lester, Kobalt)

Neil Finn & Paul Kelly

Goin' Your Way (2013) (EMI/Omnivore)

Neil Finn & Liam Finn

Lightsleeper (2018) (Inertia/PIAS)

Janis Ian & Friends

The 'Better Times' Project (2020)

Websites

www.crowdedhouse.com
www.neilfinn.com
www.fangradio.com